Milestones in Discovery and Invention

MATHEMATICS

POWERFUL PATTERNS IN NATURE AND SOCIETY

Harry Henderson

CHELSEA HOUSE
PUBLISHERS
An imprint of Infobase Publishing

MATHEMATICS: Powerful Patterns in Nature and Society

Copyright © 2007 by Harry Henderson

Chelsea House
An imprint of Infobase Publishing
132 West 31st Street
New York NY 10001

ISBN-10: 0-8160-5750-8
ISBN-13: 978-0-8160-5750-4

Library of Congress Cataloging-in-Publication Data

Henderson, Harry, 1951–
    Mathematics : powerful patterns in nature and society / Harry Henderson.
        p. cm. — (Milestones in discovery and invention)
    Includes bibliographical reference and index.
ISBN 0-8160-5750-8
1. Mathematics. 2. Mathematics—History. 3. Mathematics—Social aspects. I. Title.
    QA21.H46 2007
    510—dc22   2006024680

Chelsea House books are available at special discounts when purchased in bulk quantities for businesses, associations, institutions, or sales promotions. Please call our Special Sales Department in New York at (212) 967-8800 or (800) 322-8755.

You can find Chelsea House on the World Wide Web at http://www.chelseahouse.com

Text design by James Scotto-Lavino
Cover design by Dorothy M. Preston
Illustrations by Sholto Ainslie and Melissa Ericksen

Printed in the United States of America

MP FOF 10 9 8 7 6 5 4 3 2 1

This book is printed on acid-free paper.

CONTENTS

PREFACE

The Milestones in Discovery and Invention set is based on a simple but powerful idea—that science and technology are not separate from people's daily lives. Rather, they are part of seeking to understand and reshape the world, an activity that virtually defines being human.

More than a million years ago, the ancestors of modern humans began to shape stones into tools that helped them compete with the specialized predators around them. Starting about 35,000 years ago, the modern type of human, *Homo sapiens*, also created elaborate cave paintings and finely crafted art objects, showing that technology had been joined with imagination and language to compose a new and vibrant world of culture. Humans were not only shaping their world but representing it in art and thinking about its nature and meaning.

Technology is a basic part of that culture. The mythologies of many peoples include a trickster figure, who upsets the settled order of things and brings forth new creative and destructive possibilities. In many myths, for instance, a trickster such as the Native Americans' Coyote or Raven steals fire from the gods and gives it to human beings. All technology, whether it harnesses fire, electricity, or the energy locked in the heart of atoms or genes, partakes of the double-edged gift of the trickster, providing power to both hurt and heal.

An inventor of technology is often inspired by the discoveries of scientists. Science as we know it today is younger than technology, dating back about 500 years to a period called the Renaissance. During the Renaissance, artists and thinkers began to explore nature systematically, and the first modern scientists, such as Leonardo da Vinci (1452–1519) and Galileo Galilei (1564–1642), used instruments and experiments to develop and test ideas about how objects in the universe behaved. A succession of revolutions followed, often introduced by individual geniuses: Isaac Newton (1643–1727) in mechanics and mathematics, Charles Darwin (1809–1882) in biological evolution, Albert Einstein (1879–1955) in relativity and quantum physics, James Watson (1928–   ) and Francis Crick (1916–2004) in modern genetics. Today's emerging fields of science and technology, such as genetic engineering, nanotechnology, and artificial intelligence, have their own inspiring leaders.

The fact that particular names such as Newton, Darwin, and Einstein can be so easily associated with these revolutions suggests the importance of the individual in modern science and technology. Each book in this set thus focuses on the lives and achievements of eight to 10 individuals who together have revolutionized an aspect of science or technology. Each book presents a different field: marine science, genetics, astronomy and space science, forensic science, communications technology, robotics, artificial intelligence, and mathematical simulation. Although early pioneers are included where appropriate, the emphasis is generally on researchers who worked in the 20th century or are still working today.

The biographies in each volume are placed in an order that reflects the flow of the individuals' major achievements, but these life stories are often intertwined. The achievements of particular men and women cannot be understood without some knowledge of the times they lived in, the people they worked with, and developments that preceded their research. Newton famously remarked, "If I have seen further [than others], it is by standing on the shoulders of giants." Each scientist or inventor builds upon—or wrestles with—the work that has come before. Individual scientists and inventors also interact with others in their own laboratories and elsewhere, sometimes even partaking in vast collective efforts, such as the government and private projects that raced at the end of the 20th century to complete the description of the human genome. Scientists and inventors affect, and are affected by, economic, political, and social forces as well. The relationship between scientific and technical creativity and developments in social institutions is another important facet of this series.

A number of additional features provide further context for the biographies in these books. Each chapter includes a chronology and suggestions for further reading. In addition, a glossary and a general bibliography (including organizations and Web resources) appear at the end of each book. Several types of sidebars are also used in the text to explore particular aspects of the profiled scientists' and inventors' work:

Connections   Describes the relationship between the featured work and other scientific or technical developments.

I Was There   Presents first-hand accounts of discoveries or inventions.

Issues   Discusses scientific or ethical issues raised by the discovery or invention.

Other Scientists (or Inventors)   Describes other individuals who played an important part in the work being discussed.

Parallels   Shows parallel or related discoveries.

Social Impact   Suggests how the discovery or invention affects or might affect society and daily life.

Solving Problems   Explains how a scientist or inventor dealt with a particular technical problem or challenge.

Trends   Presents data or statistics showing how developments in a field changed over time.

Our hope is that readers will be intrigued and inspired by these stories of the human quest for understanding, exploration, and innovation. We have tried to provide the context and tools to enable readers to forge their own connections and to further pursue their fields of interest.

ACKNOWLEDGMENTS

I would like to acknowledge the help of numerous people who helped me obtain photos of the people and subjects discussed in this book. And as always, I would like to thank Frank K. Darmstadt, executive editor; Amy L. Conver, copy editor; and the rest of the editorial and production staff for their help in making this project a reality.

INTRODUCTION

The essence of mathematics is the search for patterns in observing the world and for tools that let one find or create new patterns. Some patterns people find can be useful—such as for predicting the weather. In other cases, the sheer pleasure of finding how things fit together may be enough.

Prehistoric humans were acting as mathematicians when they noticed the relationship between the length of an animal's coat and the coming of winter. With the coming of the first cities—of "civilization"—came the development of new tools for finding and using patterns. These included new ways to count, the development of number systems, procedures for calculation, and tools for measurement. The lore that became geometry could tell a farmer where his farm should be in relation to the nearest river. The priests in the local temple could observe the stars and determine when the time for planting had come. Kings and priests, of course, were also interested in collecting taxes, while traders had to be able to figure the comparative value of goods and of various forms of money.

About 2,500 years ago, some Greeks such as Pythagoras and Euclid began to pursue mathematics in a purer form. They did not ask what one could *do* with mathematics but believed that it was a discipline that could bring the mind to the understanding of the "ideal" reality that was only revealed imperfectly in the flawed world. And although the Greeks were not particularly practical, they did believe that their architecture and art should reflect the beauty revealed by mathematics, and so they embodied the "golden ratio" in their designs for buildings such as the Parthenon.

The mathematicians in this book mainly worked in the 20th century. However, what we call modern mathematics and science owed much to a flourishing Islamic civilization that stretched from the Middle East across Africa and both enticed and challenged medieval Europe. The book begins with Leonardo of Pisa, better known as Fibonacci. This 13th-century "mathematical traveler" brought what are known today as "Arabic numerals" to Europe, along with the work of Arabic mathematicians who were translating and improving on the geometry of the ancient Greeks, while inventing algebra and exploring number theory. Fibonacci's best-known achievement, though, was his exploration of the properties of a number series that has turned out to correspond to many structures found in nature, including those of many leaves and flowers. Leonardo thus provided a first gift of tools and patterns to European mathematicians.

The book then jumps to the 19th and early 20th centuries, where new techniques were being born. By then, powerful new mathematics, such as the calculus of Newton and Leibniz, was transforming natural science, particularly physics. With the industrial age in full swing and modern states looking for ways to manage a growing population and economy, vast amounts of data were being collected. What was needed, though, were the mathematical techniques that could find correlations in that data and express the degree of certainty that one might have in conclusions. The next featured mathematician, Karl Pearson, developed many of the tools used by statisticians today, even as he perhaps overreached in coming to conclusions about evolution and the perfection of society.

Around the time Pearson's career was ending, a new tool was being developed—the digital computer. John von Neumann was one of the key designers of the computer, and the essential features of his design still sit on desktops today. But von Neumann did more than develop the computer as an essential data-processing tool. He also recognized its potential as a tool for the imagination, for simulating the processes of nature as well as human interactions.

Human interactions were the main mathematical interest of John Nash, who made key discoveries in what became known as game theory. This weighing of options and searching for optimal strategy is used every day behind the scenes in labor negotiations, corporate mergers, and foreign policy. Nash, however, may have won his most important game when he used his logical skills to disarm the phantasms of schizophrenia.

The next two mathematicians opened a new portal into understanding the complexity of nature. Benoît Mandelbrot discovered the world of fractal geometry, with its intricately nested, ever-varying patterns. Today fractals are used in computer graphics, data compression, and even more esoteric applications.

Around the same time, a meteorologist named Edward Lorenz was hoping to use computer models to create more reliable weather forecasts. One day, he discovered by accident that slight changes in variables could produce wildly different results. Lorenz became the first of a generation of researchers who explored the nature of chaotic phenomena that were determined by natural laws but could not be predicted. Chaos theory has become an essential tool of modern science.

Another way to generate patterns was popularized by mathematician and puzzle master John H. Conway, who around 1970 invented a game that he called Life. In it, simple rules are used to generate complex patterns in what is called cellular automation. The fascination of watching complexity emerge from simplicity hinted at yet another way of looking at the processes of nature.

Two more researchers took that hint in different directions. Christopher Langton developed and popularized the field of artificial life, where simulated organisms interact with each other and the environment while they are subjected to Darwinian natural selection, with their computer codes serving the functions of genes. This research has now found its way into sophisticated robots and software agents.

Stephen Wolfram has undertaken an even more ambitious project. A brilliant young physicist, he turned his attention to mathematical computing and cellular automation in the 1980s, and in the 1990s, he worked secretively on a "theory of everything." His 2002 book, *A New Kind of Science,* makes bold claims that nature can be better understood by identifying patterns and their underlying rules rather than through the traditional method of fitting equations to observations. Only time will tell whether Wolfram's work represents a true scientific revolution.

Finally, there is Roger Penrose, the mathematical physicist who worked with Stephen Hawking to understand the nature of black holes and their interaction with energy and information. Penrose has also tried to sketch out possible connections between the tiny world of quanta and the sweeping arena of relativity. Within this vast pattern, Penrose speculates on the nature of the human mind and consciousness and suggests that they can exploit quantum processes to understand the world in a way that cannot be matched by the brute force of ever more powerful computer chips.

It should be said that the selection of mathematicians for this volume is necessarily a bit arbitrary. There are many other significant pattern-finders and pattern-makers in the history of modern mathematics—though not all may be equally accessible to the non-mathematician. The author has therefore emphasized mathematical thinkers whose ideas are provocative, intriguing, and continuing to resonate in today's science and technology.

1
HOW NATURE COUNTS

LEONARDO OF PISA DISCOVERS FIBONACCI NUMBERS

Around the year 1170, a boy named Leonardo was born near the town of Pisa in northern Italy. Following the usage of the time, he was usually called Leonardo Pisano, or Leonardo of Pisa. However, his father, Guglielmo (William), had been given the nickname "Bonacci," meaning "good-natured." In his later writings, Leonardo would become best known by the nickname "Fibonacci," meaning "filio Bonacci," or "son of Bonacci." Leonardo would play a key role in taking European mathematics from the Middle Ages to the Renaissance, and his lasting legacy would be a remarkable series of numbers.

When Leonardo was 12, his father was appointed as a representative of Italian merchants in the port of Bugia (now Bougie) on the north coast of what is now

Leonardo of Pisa, nicknamed "Fibonacci," brought state-of-the-art Arab mathematics to medieval Europe. He also discovered and popularized a remarkable series of numbers that have many correspondences in nature. (SPL/ Photo Researchers, Inc.)

1

Algeria. The expansion of a vigorous and sophisticated Arabic culture in North Africa brought trading opportunities for the growing Italian merchant class. It also offered the opportunity for Europeans to learn from Arab mathematicians who had preserved much ancient knowledge that had been lost in Europe since the fall of the Roman Empire hundreds of years earlier. Young Leonardo's source of instruction was only a local schoolmaster, but that was apparently sufficient to provide him with a good background in mathematics and a love of the discipline.

Those Useful Arabic Numerals

The Italian merchants typified by Leonardo's family were on their way to becoming Europe's first "modern" bankers, but they faced a serious obstacle when it came to doing basic arithmetic. The Roman numerals in use at the time used letters to stand for particular numbers: I (1), V (5), X (10), L (50), C (100), and so on. These numbers were simply lumped together, such that XXX, for example, was 30, or occasionally subtracted (as with IX for 9).

Working with Roman numerals was difficult. To perform calculations, numbers such as CCCXC (390) or MDCL (1,650) had to be "disassembled" into their component parts and then grouped and converted back to a single numeral. If addition and subtraction were merely painful, multiplication and division with Roman numerals must have been excruciating! New forms of business such as banks and joint-stock companies required sophisticated bookkeeping, and that, in turn, required a better way of doing arithmetic. Fortunately, an alternative was about to become available.

Leonardo later recalled in his 1202 book *Liber Abaci* (The book of counting, or calculation) that

When my father, who had been appointed by his country as public notary in the customs at Bugia acting for the Pisan merchants going there, was in charge, he summoned me to him while I was still a child, and having an eye to usefulness and future convenience, desired me to stay there and receive instruction in the school of accounting. There, when I had been introduced to the art of the Indians' nine symbols through remarkable teaching, knowledge of the art very soon pleased me above all else and I came to understand it, for whatever was studied by the art in Egypt, Syria, Greece, Sicily and Provence [a region in France], in all its various forms.

Originally developed in India, this system of 10 numerals (including the essential placeholder, zero) greatly simplified calculation. In *Liber Abaci*, Leonardo publicized what came to be known as Arabic numerals: "These are the nine figures of the Indians: 9, 8, 7, 6, 5, 4, 3, 2, 1. With these nine figures, and the sign 0 . . . any number may be written, as will be demonstrated."

Because it used a system of places (tens, hundreds, and so on), the system was well suited to performing arithmetic by moving beads or counters, "carrying" one over to the left for each group of 10. This positional system (and its revolutionary use of a placeholder zero) took some getting used to. With his second edition of *Liber Abaci* in 1228, Leonardo made a substantial contribution to the gradual adoption of the new system, particularly by businesses, over the next two centuries.

Practical Mathematics

Leonardo's book also introduced Europeans to a number of developments in Arab mathematics, including methods for solving simultaneous linear equations, where the value of a variable can be determined through its relationships to other variables.

The wide-ranging *Liber Abaci* also included methods for solving practical business problems. For example, as businesses grew, it became important to keep track of all expenses in order to determine how much profit one was actually making in a given transaction. Leonardo provided procedures for calculating profits. Another common problem Leonardo dealt with was the conversion of one currency to another, an essential task at a time when "pocket change" might include coins from a dozen different nations or city-states. Similarly, systems of weights and measures were also far from uniform, requiring conversion in order to determine a fair price.

Reviving Mathematics in Europe

After returning to Pisa around 1200, Leonardo began to write about mathematics. In addition to *Liber Abaci,* Leonardo wrote a number of other books. Since printing did not yet exist, all books had to be written and copied by hand. Titles that survive today include *Practica geometriae* (Practical geometry). This book contains a large selection of geometry problems based on the theorems explored by Euclid. The book also provided practical procedures for surveyors, including a method to use similar triangles to calculate the height of a distant object.

Leonardo's work became well known in the intellectual community of the time. Even Frederick II, the Holy Roman Emperor, met with Leonardo and other intellectuals when his court met in Pisa around 1225.

During that meeting, a courtier named Johannes of Palermo posed a number of mathematical problems to challenge Leonardo. Leonardo solved three of the problems and published the solutions in his book *Flos,* which he presented to Frederick II. In 1240, the Republic of Pisa issued a proclamation awarding the mathematician an annual salary.

Here is an example problem from the third section of *Liber Abaci:*

If a spider climbs X feet up a wall each day and always slips back Y feet each night (with Y being less than X), how many days would it take the spider to climb a wall Z feet high?

(There is a trick to this problem. While the spider climbs a net of X - Y feet each day, when it gets to within X feet of the top of the wall, it will be able to reach the top without slipping back.)

Number Theory

Leonardo's book *Liber Quadratorum* (The book of squares) is his most important work in terms of pure mathematics. It deals pri-

OTHER MATHEMATICIANS: ARAB MATHEMATICIANS

Much of ancient Greek mathematics (including geometry) had been lost or forgotten in Europe by the time of the Middle Ages. Meanwhile, however, a sophisticated and vigorous Islamic culture had spread through the Middle East, Africa, and even Spain and central Europe. This culture used Arabic as its international language, much as Latin was used in Europe.

Arabic mathematics drew on the work of ancient Greeks, such as the great geometer Euclid. Indeed, many ancient Greek mathematics texts are known today only because they were preserved and translated by Arabic scholars.

One of the most important contributions of Arabic mathematics to the world was the promotion of the base-10 positional numeric systems, now called "Arabic numerals." This system was promoted by al-Khwarizmi (c. 780–850), a Persian mathematician and astronomer who served the caliph of Baghdad. In Latin translation, this writer's work used the phrase "dixit Algorismi" or "so says al-Khwarizmi," and from that comes the modern word *algorithm* to describe a computational procedure.

Probably the most famous Arabic name in mathematics comes from the title of one of al-Khwarizmi's works, *Kitab al-jabr wa al-muqabalah,* which described how to set up equations and find the value of an unknown variable. From *Al-Jabr* came a word that has struck fear into the heart of many a high school student: *algebra.*

As European scholarship began to revive in the 12th and 13th centuries, scholars began to learn Arabic in order to translate the Arabic versions of the lost Greek texts of mathematics and philosophy into Latin. (They were also aided by Jewish scholars from the Middle East who already knew Arabic.) It was in this way that much of the writings of Euclid and the other Greeks, as well as new Arabic works on algebra, found their way into the new universities of Europe.

marily with what today is called number theory, or the properties and patterns of numbers. In particular, Leonardo looked at "square numbers" (numbers such as 4 and 9 that are the product of a smaller number multiplied by itself.) Leonardo presented a way to construct sets of square numbers called "Pythagorean triples."

Many people will remember from geometry class that the ancient Greek mathematician and mystic Pythagoras proved that in a triangle containing a right (90-degree) angle, the square of the length of the hypotenuse (the long diagonal side) is equal to the sum of the squares of the other two sides. A Pythagorean triple is simply a set of three numbers that have that same relationship (the first such triple is 3, 4, 5 since their squares are 9, 16, and 25, respectively).

In *Liber Quadratorum*, Leonardo notes how he discovered the secret to constructing square numbers:

I thought about the origin of all square numbers and discovered that they arose from the regular ascent of odd numbers. For unity [one] is a square and from it is produced the first square, namely 1; adding 3 to this makes the second square, namely 4, whose root is 2; if to this sum is added a third odd number, namely 5, the third square will be produced, namely 9, whose root is 3; and so the sequence and series of square numbers always rise through the regular addition of odd numbers.

Leonardo then explained how to construct the Pythagorean triples:

Thus when I wish to find two square numbers whose addition produces a square number, I take any odd square number as one of the two square numbers and I find the other square number by the addition of all the odd numbers from unity [one] up to but excluding the odd square number. For example, I take 9 as one of the two squares mentioned; the remaining square will be obtained by the addition of all the odd numbers below 9, namely 1, 3, 5, 7, whose sum is 16, a square number, which when added to 9 gives 25, a square number.

Leonardo also proved other number theorems, such as the impossibility of there being an X and Y such that both $X^2 + Y^2$ and $X^2 - Y^2$ are themselves squares.

A Problem with Rabbits

Leonardo's work in number theory is seen today as a crucial link between the achievements of ancient mathematicians such as Diophantus and later Europeans such as Pierre Fermat. Leonardo's most memorable achievement, however, came from a problem that he described in the third section of *Liber Abaci*: "A certain man put a pair of rabbits in a place surrounded on all sides by a wall. How many pairs of rabbits can be produced from that pair in a year if it is supposed that every month each pair begets a new pair which from the second month on becomes productive?"

As shown in the accompanying diagram, the results can be summarized as a numeric sequence (beginning with two ones) where each subsequent number is equal to the sum of the preceding two numbers: 1, 1, 2, 3, 5, 8, 13, and so on. This simple series of numbers turned out to have surprising significance in many areas.

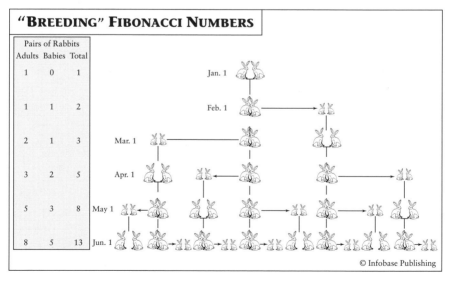

© Infobase Publishing

Start with one pair of adult (breeding) rabbits. For the sake of argument, assume that each adult pair produces one pair of baby bunnies each month. The babies take one month to reach breeding age. The resulting count of pairs of adult and baby rabbits turns out to match the Fibonacci series.

Although this number series was apparently known in India since around the ninth century, Leonardo placed it in a larger context and publicized it in the wider mathematical world.

Fibonacci Numbers in Nature

A few centuries after Leonardo's time, the period called the Renaissance was under way. Artists and scientists began to look closely at the natural world, including the structures of plants and the bodies of animals and humans. As they began to study these structures, something remarkable happened: Fibonacci numbers began to turn up in the measurements!

For example, plants grow in such a way as to use each seasonal "burst" of energy and resources to follow and move toward life-giving sunlight and moisture. The result is a spiral structure in which each segment is a certain length, allowing leaves to be spaced so they capture sunlight without blocking one another. It turns out that these "phyllotactic ratios" generally correspond to the Fibonacci number series. Similar ratios occur in the spirals found in pinecones, artichokes, and the centers of daisies and sunflowers.

The spiral structure of this daisy turns out to progress along a Fibonacci sequence. Many other plant structures contain Fibonacci numbers. (Public domain photo, www.pdphoto.com)

Similar spirals can be found in the growth of animals. Rather than consisting of evenly spaced segments, the beautiful spiral shell of the chambered nautilus consists of an "equiangular spiral" where the internal angle remains the same as the segments into which the growing animal moves, getting progressively larger, following a fixed ratio. This same structure can be seen in starfish, sand dollars, and even many types of spiderwebs. (While not all such structures yield Fibonacci numbered ratios, many do.)

The Golden Ratio

Fibonacci numbers also turn up in the things people build. Perhaps because of its connection to growth and its widespread appearance in nature, ratios based on the Fibonacci sequence were featured in the architecture of the ancient world. The segments of the famous Greek temple the Parthenon, for example, form so-called golden rectangles.

The golden rectangle has a particular ratio. The ratio of the smaller side to the larger side is the same as the ratio of the larger side to the combined lengths. That is, if a rectangle has a width of A and a length of B, then A is to B as B is to (A + B).

If one takes succeeding pairs of numbers in the Fibonacci sequence, one gets closer and closer to the golden ratio. Thus in the series 1, 1, 2, 3, 5, 8, 13, 21, 34, 55, 89, 144, 233, 13/21 = 0.619047, while 144/233 equals 0.618037. Each successive ratio between higher pairs of Fibonacci numbers more closely approximates the "ideal" golden ratio of 0.618034.

Scholars who have examined ancient architecture find golden ratios (also called golden sections) in many places where the ratios of sides of rectangles come to either 0.618 or its inverse, 1.618. Sometimes the ratio is only an approximation, such as 3/5 (0.6) or 5/8 (0.625), but these approximations convey about the same impression to the human eye. Golden ratios also turn up in modern architecture (such as the United Nations building in New York) and in paintings, from the Renaissance to 19th-century Impressionists and beyond. The pleasing properties of the golden ratio are even found in humble items such as the three-by-five and five-by-eight-inch index card.

Musical scales, too, are related to Fibonacci numbers. The most familiar one, the diatonic scale, uses an octave (eight notes). Much folk music is based on a pentatonic (five-tone) scale, while sophisti-

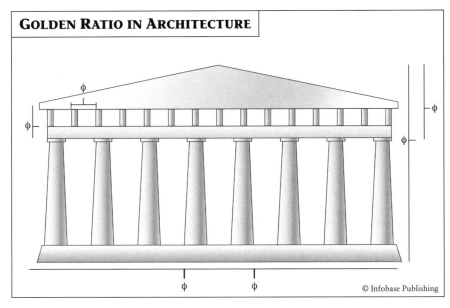

The golden ratio (denoted by the Greek letter φ) seems to be aesthetically and psychologically pleasing. Here it shows up in several parts of the Parthenon of ancient Greece.

cated classical and contemporary music uses a chromatic (13-note) scale (5, 8, and 13 are of course Fibonacci numbers).

An Inner Harmony?

In the late 19th century, Gustav Fechner, a German psychologist, measured many rectangles found in common signs, labels, and other uses. The majority of them approximated the golden ratio. Fechner also tested the reactions of hundreds of people to golden and random rectangles and found a strong preference for the former. Modern designers of signs, labels, and even Web sites have taken note.

Why do people prefer the golden ratio and golden rectangle? Perhaps it is because they see so much of it in nature that it feels comfortable and natural. It could be that the nervous system is somehow hard-wired to respond favorably to such ratios. Much

PARALLELS: MATHEMATICS AND GREEK PHILOSOPHY

The discovery of number patterns and geometric ratios in nature would not have surprised ancient Greek thinkers such as Pythagoras and Plato. Pythagoras (582 B.C.–507 B.C.) founded a school of mystical philosophy based on his idea that every aspect of nature was based on mathematics. Indeed, to the Pythagoreans, it was mathematics that was the true reality. Nature was perceived as simply a reflection and approximation of mathematical truth.

As a young man, Pythagoras went to Egypt, where he probably learned some of the basic principles of geometry on which he would build conclusions such as the famous Pythagorean theorem, which states that in a right triangle the square of the length of the hypotenuse is equal to the sum of the squares of the other two sides. When Pythagoras returned to the Greek city of Crotone and founded his school, his students called themselves *mathematikoi* (disciples), from which the word *mathematics* is derived. The Pythagoreans mixed their mathematical knowledge with meditation, arcane rituals, and strange prohibitions (such as not eating beans, which they believed contained tiny human embryos). The Pythagoreans also placed much value on music, having discovered the relationship between musical intervals and the ratios between whole numbers.

The Greek philosopher Plato (c. 427 B.C.–347 B.C.) was likely influenced by the ideas of Pythagoras. Just as Pythagoras taught that true reality was mathematical, Plato distinguished between perfect "ideas" and their imperfect realization in the perceived "forms" in nature. This type of philosophy is sometimes called dualism because of its division between the thinking intellect and the sensing body.

By his exploration of numeric series and his conscious application of the golden ratio, Leonardo of Pisa helped point European thinkers toward the Pythagorean and Platonic idea that mathematics underlay the structures of nature and human artifice. However, while many of the ancient Greek thinkers believed that mathematics was to be pursued only within the mind (with the minimal assistance of a few geometrical tools), in the centuries following Leonardo of Pisa, scientists would begin to marry mathematics to a systematic process of observing the details of natural phenomena.

research remains to be done, but it is clear that ancient architects and medieval mathematicians such as Leonardo of Pisa recognized the power of numbers and their relationships to describe nature to enhance art and architecture.

Leonardo's Legacy

Leonardo of Pisa, the Fibonacci numbers, and the golden ratios were a sort of mathematical bridge from ancient times to the modern world. Although little is known of the details of the life of this mathematical pioneer, the circulation of his writings helped foster a new interest in both mathematics and the observation and exploration of nature. This curiosity about the structures of the world (including the human world) would define the period called the Renaissance (roughly, the 14th and 15th centuries, beginning in Italy and spreading throughout Europe and England).

The structural beauty and explanatory power of mathematics would play a key role in the evolution of new understanding in art, architecture, engineering, the physical sciences, and medicine. The simple patterns and ratios found by Leonardo of Pisa were only a taste of mathematical realms to come.

Chronology

582 B.C.– **507 B.C.**	Pythagoras founds a school of mathematics and mystical philosophy based on the idea that true reality is embodied in numbers
427 B.C.– **347 B.C.**	The philosopher Plato bases his dualistic philosophy on the distinction between perfect "ideas," akin to geometrical figures, and their imperfect "forms," as perceived in the world
	The Greek Parthenon, built at about this time, embodies the geometrical "golden ratio"
780–850	The Persian mathematician al-Khwarizmi introduces Indian numerals into the Islamic world and develops algebra (named for one of his works)

1170	Approximate birth date of Leonardo in Pisa, Italy
1180s	Leonardo travels with his father to Algeria, where he is tutored in Arabic mathematics by a schoolmaster
1202	Having returned to Italy, Leonardo publishes *Liber Abaci*, introducing Indian numerals (now called Arabic numerals) to Europe
1225	Leonardo publishes *Liber Quadratorum*, the first major European work in number theory
1228	Leonardo publishes a second, expanded edition of *Liber Abaci*
1240	Approximate death date of Leonardo of Pisa
1300s and 1400s	The Renaissance brings mathematics into art, architecture, and the beginnings of modern science

Further Reading

Books

Garland, Trudi Hammel. *Fascinating Fibonaccis: Mystery and Magic in Numbers.* Parsippany, N.J.: Dale Seymour Publications (Pearson Learning Group), 1987.
> A very accessible and well-illustrated account of many aspects of Fibonacci numbers.

Gies, Joseph, and Frances Gies. *Leonard of Pisa and the New Mathematics of the Middle Ages.* Gainesville, Ga.: New Classics Library, 1983.
> Describes the life and work of Leonardo of Pisa and its influence on the development of Western mathematics.

Livio, Mario. *The Golden Ratio: The Story of Phi, the World's Most Astonishing Number.* New York: Broadway Books, 2003.
> An engaging account of the discovery and prolific appearances of phi, the "golden ratio" in nature, architecture, and symbolism.

Vorobiev, Nicolai N. *Fibonacci Numbers.* Boston: Birkäuser Verlag, 2002.
> A more technical survey of the properties of Fibonacci numbers, beginning with fundamentals and the "rabbit problem."

Articles

O'Connor, J.J., and E. F. Robertson. "Arabic Mathematics: Forgotten Brilliance?" University of St. Andrews, Scotland. School of Mathematics and Statistics. Available online. URL: http://www.history.mcs.st-andrews.ac.uk/HistTopics/Arabic_mathematics.html. Posted in January 2004.

> Describes Arabic mathematicians and their work from the eighth to the 15th centuries.

Web Sites

Fibonacci Association. Available online. URL: http://www.mscs.dal.ca/Fibonacci. Accessed on July 24, 2006.

> Provides links to background and research on Fibonacci numbers and related math.

Fibonacci Numbers and the Golden Section. Dr. Ron Knott. Available online. URL: http://www.mcs.surrey.ac.uk/Personal/R.Knott/Fibonacci/fib.html. Accessed July 2, 2006.

> An award-winning Web site with numerous links to explanations, illustrations, applications, and puzzles involving Fibonacci numbers and phi (the "golden section").

2
TOOLS FOR PATTERN-FINDERS

KARL PEARSON AND STATISTICS

According to a biographical sketch by Helen M. Walker, the first thing Karl Pearson recalled from his early childhood was someone telling him that he better stop sucking his thumb or it would wither away. Sitting in his high chair, little Karl put his thumbs alongside each other and studied them carefully. He concluded that the thumb he had been sucking was no shorter than its companion. The boy decided that the evidence did not support the adult's claim. Karl Pearson would grow up to become one of the founders of modern statistics, the tool scientists use to determine the significance of observations and experiments.

A Roving Mind

Karl Pearson was born in London, England, on March 27, 1857. His father, William, was a barrister (attorney), and the family was relatively prosperous. Pearson's father was a fierce believer in the power of education, urging Karl and his older brother Arthur to study hard, saying that it was the only sure road to success later in life. However, William and his wife, Fanny, had a stormy relationship, with the boys taking the side of their more vulnerable mother.

Karl Pearson developed many of the basic statistical methods used in modern physical and social science. However, his involvement in the eugenics movement was controversial. (© Topham/Fotomas/The Image Works)

Young Pearson was a bright student, though his health was delicate. As a teenager, he spent a lonely season in a country school where he had been sent to be prepared for university. In 1875, however, Pearson had the opportunity to study with E. J. Routh, one of the foremost mathematical "coaches" of the day. Pearson was not well prepared for tutoring by someone who normally taught advanced college students, but he did acquire from Routh an interest in the mathematics of elasticity, a topic in physics that would prove to be Pearson's main mathematical interest until he became involved with statistics.

Although he failed the entrance exam for Trinity College at Cambridge University, Pearson persevered and won admission to the university's King's College, his second choice. There Pearson majored in mathematics and came in third highest in the arduous series of examinations called the Tripos. However, King's College actually featured literature and the humanities more than math and science, and Pearson became increasingly interested in philosophy—particularly German philosophy.

Pearson's academic performance resulted in a fellowship to pay for further studies in Germany, but he did not limit his interests to mathematics. Besides qualifying to practice law in 1881, Pearson also studied physics, biology, history, classic German literature, art, social and political science, and philosophy. He also encountered the work of Karl Marx, whose economic theories impressed Pearson so much that he changed his first name from Carl to Karl. All in all, Pearson's wide-ranging intellect showed him to be a renaissance person whose curiosity was accompanied by the discipline needed to master one field after another.

After returning to London with his doctorate, the enthusiastic Pearson organized a Young Men's and Women's Discussion Club. Rather like the fashionable intellectual salons of Paris, the club allowed young men and women to discuss the political and philosophical issues of the day without being hindered by the chaperones upon which the Victorian Age usually insisted. Pearson lectured on topics ranging from Martin Luther to the philosophy of Spinoza to the socialism of Karl Marx. Pearson also benefited from the salon's abundant social opportunities; through the salon, he met and married his wife, Maria Sharpe, in 1890.

Pearson's broad foundations in the humanities as well as science would also be seen in his varied writings. He wrote a novel, a play, and a number of essays that appeared in collections with titles such as *Ethic of Freethought* (1888) and *Chances of Death and Other Studies of Evolution* (1897).

The Grammar of Science

In 1884, Pearson began his academic career as Professor of Applied Mathematics and Mechanics at University College, London. "Mechanics" meant the study of the behavior of physical systems, and Pearson took over the task of completing a book on the history of the theory of elasticity. He also took over and finished a book called *Common Sense in the Exact Sciences,* which was intended to explain the role of mathematics in science to undergraduate students. This book was highly regarded and would be republished in 1946 with a new preface by one of its most prominent fans, the great philosopher and mathematician Bertrand Russell. Meanwhile, Pearson's academic career progressed steadily. In 1907, he became head of the university's Department of Applied Mathematics.

Common Sense was an example of Pearson's lifelong interest in the nature of science and scientific method. That interest would culminate in Pearson's own book, *Grammar of Science*, being published in 1892. In it, Pearson defines the scientific method as "the orderly classification of facts followed by the recognition of their relationship and recurring sequences."

Pearson's *Grammar of Science* would inspire many young scientists and students of scientific method in the first half of the 20th century. However, the book was rather shocking at a time when much of science involved citing and giving great respect to past authorities. In 1915, Russian student and future statistician Jerzy Neyman and his fellow students were reading Pearson's book in translation. As recounted in an article by Richard Williams, Neyman recalled that

---

OTHER SCIENTISTS: FRANCIS GALTON

Francis Galton (1822–1911) studied both mathematics and medicine as a young man and then became well known as an African explorer and geographer. Returning to England and resuming his academic career, Galton became intensely interested in the measurement of human characteristics, as well as providing mathematical support for the theory of evolution introduced by his cousin Charles Darwin.

Galton's statistical work focused on the so-called normal distribution or "bell curve" that expresses the typical way in which a large series of measurements ends up being arranged. He also explained an idea called regression to the mean, in which an unusually high or low measurement is more likely to be followed by one closer to the mean, or average. (For example, very tall people tend to have children who are still tall, but shorter than their parents.) Finally, Galton introduced the term *coefficient of correlation* for a calculation of the degree of regression to the mean.

Galton's more controversial side was seen in his support for eugenics, or the idea that humans with superior qualities should be encouraged to marry in order to steadily improve the human race, while people who were inferior or below average should be discouraged from reproducing.

Galton's most unusual legacy can be seen every week on *CSI* and other crime shows. Galton pointed out that fingerprints were very likely unique and thus could be used for identification or the linking of a suspect to a crime scene.

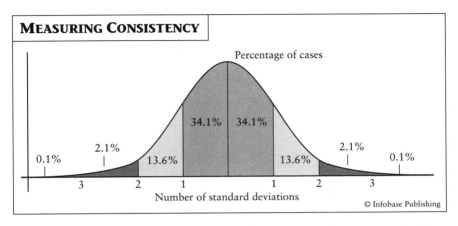

MEASURING CONSISTENCY

Percentage of cases

34.1% 34.1%

2.1% 2.1%

0.1% 0.1%

13.6% 13.6%

3   2   1   1   2   3

Number of standard deviations

© Infobase Publishing

Standard deviation is a key concept in modern statistics. It measures the dispersion or consistency of data or measurements. In the normal distribution or "bell curve," about 95 percent of data will fall within two standard deviations of the mean.

The reading of The Grammar of Science was striking because . . . it attacked in an uncompromising manner all sorts of authorities. . . . At the first reading it was this aspect that struck us. What could it mean? We had been unused to this tone in any scientific book. Was the work . . . [something of a hoax] and the author a . . . [scoundrel] on a grand scale?

Pearson's focus on scientific method would also shape his later mathematical work. The process of finding and testing patterns and relationships is a statistician's job. As a mathematician, Pearson would develop some of the most important tools used by statisticians in every field of science and technology today.

Statistical Tools

Although Pearson's interests were many and varied, he gradually began to focus on the mathematical approach to biology and, particularly, to evolution and the emerging science of genetics. Over the course of his career, he would write more than 300 publications.

Of these, his 18 papers for the *Transactions of the Royal Society* on various aspects of "Mathematical Contributions to the Theory of Evolution" would contain Pearson's most important contributions to statistical methodology.

Galton and other pioneer statisticians had begun to discover that there were often patterns in how (and how much) measurements varied. As scientific experiments became more elaborate (and observations in the biological and social sciences became more extensive), it was increasingly important to determine just how much one could learn from those experiments and measurements.

Unlike the ideal world of mathematical plotting, the real world was filled with measurements that might be approximations of the true value or freakish outliers that might have to be discarded. Pearson developed a way to plot curves that expressed the probability that a given value might turn up in a measurement. Put another way, he developed a way to bridge between ideal and reality, showing the pattern within the seeming randomness of even the most careful measurements.

Pearson was thus able to measure the measurements. In doing so, he was able to determine four key parameters:

- The mean, or the central or most common value around which all the others scatter (this is the fattest part of the bell curve)
- The standard deviation, or a measurement of the degree to which measurements scatter at various distances from the mean
- The amount of symmetry, or the degree to which measurements are either evenly distributed or tend to pile up on one side or the other of the mean
- Kurtosis, or the distance of the occasional far-off outliers from the mean

While later researchers found that there were limitations to Pearson's system and a number of situations to which it could not be applied, Pearson's analysis of distribution allowed for the development of the basic tools of modern statistics.

In addition to studying the distribution of measurements, Pearson made a key contribution to the problem of determining how well the observed results of an experiment corresponded to the values predicted by theory. (This was an essential part of showing whether a given experiment had yielded evidence for a particular theory or hypothesis.) Pearson's goodness of fit test became known as "chi squared," from the Greek letter used as a symbol of the value. This and more sophisticated tests are what modern statisticians use in order to determine whether a result is significant and unlikely to be due to chance.

In 1900, Pearson, together with Francis Galton and Walter Weldon, founded the journal *Biometrika*. This title consists of two Greek words: *bios* ("life," as in biology) and *metric,* or measurement. The journal's purpose was to promote the statistical study of biology, particularly evolution and heredity. However, the influence of this work would extend not only to the biological sciences but also to the physical and social sciences. Pearson realized that the statistical tools he was developing could be applied to any field involving observation and experimentation.

Eugenics and the Galton Laboratory

In 1907, Pearson inherited a research laboratory that had been founded by Galton and reorganized it as the Francis Galton

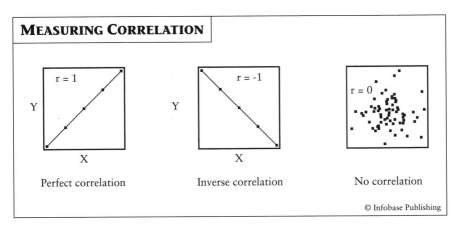

Pearson's correlation formula shows the relationship between variables. A value of 1 indicates perfect correlation (the variables rise or fall together). A value of -1 indicates inverse correlation (one goes up as the other goes down). Finally, a value of 0 would mean that there is no correlation at all between the variables in question.

ISSUES: EVALUATING EXPERIMENTS

Modern experimental science would be impossible without the use of sophisticated statistical tools.

Data are not gathered in a vacuum. Normally, scientists decide to conduct an experiment or survey because they have a hypothesis they want to prove or disprove. For example, researchers may seek to confirm how well a program to help the homeless is working or determine the safety and efficacy of a new drug.

Whatever the goal of the research project, the theories, hopes, and expectations brought to the measuring process are likely to have considerable influence on what is measured, how it is measured, and what standards will be used to draw any conclusions.

The principle safeguard against scientific self-deception is the peer review process. Before a study is published in a reputable journal, experienced scientists in the same field who have no connection with the work are asked to review it. They look at how the experiment or survey is designed. For example, many experiments are designed in a double-blind format in which neither the experimenters nor the experimental subjects are told, for example, whether a test drug or an inert placebo is being administered. Reviewers look at the protocols, or procedures, of the experiment to try to identify possible sources of bias or inaccuracy.

Reviewers can also examine the statistical procedures used to analyze the results of the experiment. They ask whether all the variables likely to have an influence on the result are being controlled for or taken into account. Tools based on Pearson's ideas can also be used to examine whether the observed results fall into the expected distribution. Finally, the statistical tests used to determine significance can be examined. When a report says that a result is statistically significant, this generally means that the probability of the result being due to mere chance or some unknown factor is very small.

Laboratory of National Eugenics. Eugenics (meaning "good or happy birth") has a long but controversial history.

By the early 20th century, Darwin's theory of evolution had become well accepted by scientists. Darwin's central idea was that those members of a species who were best able to survive predators and environmental hazards would be the ones who reproduced, passing their characteristics on to the next generation.

Although scientists of the time did not yet understand the biochemical basis of heredity (particularly the role of the DNA

ISSUES: THE POLITICAL USE OF SCIENCE

In making measurements for their eugenics studies, Galton and Pearson tried to be very careful in evaluating evidence. Indeed, they established standards for significance that are still used routinely today. Nevertheless, their measurements were shaped by their theories about intelligence and other human capabilities, and many of these theories would be considered wrong or at least overly simplistic today.

As practiced by Galton and Pearson, eugenics was intended to be a humane project that would lead to a steady improvement in the health, capabilities, and happiness of humankind. However, many of the assumptions used to judge human "fitness" were questionable. Further, the terms used to describe human characteristics tended to value qualities supposedly associated with Europeans over those identified with other racial groups.

Beyond the issue of scientific validity, there was also the question of ethics and rights. Does any government or agency have the right to tell people whether or not they could have children? This question became far more than academic when policies encouraging birth control or even sterilization were applied to racial and ethnic minorities. Ultimately, the Nazis carried eugenics to a horrific conclusion through programs in which they forcibly sterilized the mentally and physically "unfit," and then went on to so-called euthanasia and, ultimately, genocide.

Scientific findings often become part of political discourse. When that happens, there are often claims that go well beyond what the scientific evidence may justify. At other times, however, strong scientific evidence may be ignored or minimized, as has been argued by critics of government policies toward global warming and climate change.

molecule), they did know that organisms carried genes that were associated with various characteristics (such as the color of the eyes or a pattern of fur). The little-known work of the monk Gregor Mendel on plant genetics had been rediscovered, allowing for basic calculations of the chance that a given characteristic of one or both parents would be passed to the offspring. Mathematical genetics was also accompanied by the experience of farmers and ranchers who had developed rough but useful methods for culling out defective plants or animals and trying to ensure that only the highest-quality ones were used for breeding.

Darwin had shown that human beings, despite their unique intellectual achievements, were animals subject to the same laws of natural selection as other creatures. The founder of the science of eugenics, Francis Galton, and successors such as Pearson set out to measure precisely hundreds of peoples' physical characteristics and to observe how they were transmitted from generation to generation. Where this attempt at a descriptive science became most controversial was when it was adopted as a form of social activism. Many eugenicists advocated policies such as screening people for inherited diseases or defects, encouraging so-called genetically superior people to procreate, while reducing the reproduction of so-called genetically inferior people through birth control or, in extreme cases, sterilization.

Pearson believed that his role as a scientist was to try to determine the facts about human heredity, not to formulate social policy. He did not live to see the worst of the Nazi racist atrocities. However, toward the end of his life, Pearson did write a paper in which he demolished the idea of "race" as used by the Nazis and some of the more extreme eugenicists.

Later Life

In his later career, Pearson's prickly personality began to have a negative effect on the development of new statistical research. As editor of *Biometrika*, Pearson was the key gatekeeper who controlled access to publicity and thus to career advancement for young researchers. Pearson had strong opinions about what kinds of research were worthwhile and who should get credit. As the science writer J. B. S. Haldane noted in a lecture about Pearson's work:

> *All power corrupts! It is impossible to be a professor in charge of an important department, and the editor of an important journal, without being somewhat corrupted. We can now see that in both capacities Pearson made mistakes. He rejected lines of research which later turned out to be fruitful. He used his own energy and that of his subordinates in research which turned out to be much less important than he believed.*

Pearson's stultifying impact on the later development of statistics is perhaps most clearly seen in his relations with R. A. Fisher, one of the most prominent statisticians of the early 20th century. Despite the fact that Fisher had done much original work on topics that were close to Pearson's heart, the older scientist snubbed him. Finally, Pearson offered Fisher a post at the Galton Laboratory, but only on the condition that he could control the topics that Fisher researched and lectured on.

When Fisher rejected the offer and separately published an important paper on the distribution and correlation of measurements, Pearson rashly rejected it. Later, he pressured the editors of *The Journal of the Royal Statistical Society* to reject another paper by Fisher. At the same time, Pearson could be polite and magnanimous when entertaining colleagues such as mathematician Jerzy Neyman. Pearson's harsh behavior seemed to arise only when he thought he was being challenged intellectually.

As new researchers (including Pearson's son Egon) began to move into the forefront, Pearson began to slip out of the mainstream. He died in 1936, just a few years before computers would revolutionize the calculation and display of statistics.

For many modern students, Pearson has been known only for "chi squared" and some footnotes for distribution formulas in textbooks. However, in recent years, there has been renewed interest in this paradoxical thinker. Biographers such as Theodore Porter have highlighted the complexities of a humanist and philosophical romantic who ended up spending his career in the world of measurements and formulas.

Chronology

1857	Karl Pearson is born in London on March 27
1879	Pearson graduates from King's College, Cambridge, with high honors in mathematics
1881	Pearson completes his law studies and is admitted to the bar
1882	Pearson travels in Germany and studies a variety of subjects, including philosophy, physics, and German literature; he receives a master's degree
1884	Pearson becomes Professor of Applied Mathematics and Mechanics at University College, London
1890	Pearson begins work on "biometrics," or statistical biology
1892	Pearson publishes *The Grammar of Science*
1896	Pearson is elected to the Royal Society
1900	Pearson, Francis Galton, and W. F. R. Weldon found the journal *Biometrika* to study biology and evolution using statistical methods
1903	Pearson establishes the Biometric Laboratory
1907	Pearson reconstitutes Galton's laboratory as the Francis Galton Laboratory of National Eugenics
1911	Pearson becomes Galton Professor of Eugenics, a post he will hold until his retirement
1933	Pearson retires
1936	Pearson dies on April 27

Further Reading

Books

Gigerenzer, Gerd [and others], eds. *The Empire of Chance: How Probability Changed Science and Everyday Life.* New York: Cambridge University Press, 1990.

Describes the revolution in science, technology, and society brought about by the understanding of probability and statistical methods.

Salsburg, David. *The Lady Tasting Tea: How Statistics Revolutionized Science in the Twentieth Century.* New York: W. H. Freeman, 2001.
Contains engaging biographical sketches and stories featuring the surprising implications of statistical techniques.

Articles

Aldrich, John. "Karl Pearson: A Reader's Guide." University of Southampton (UK). Available online. URL: http://www.economics.soton.ac.uk/staff/aldrich/kpreader.htm. Accessed on July 10, 2006.
A rich source of biographical and bibliographical information about Karl Pearson, his work, and his legacy.

Haldane, J. B. S. "Karl Pearson, 1857–1957." *Biometrika* 44 (1957): 303–313.
A lecture given on the centenary of Pearson's birth that assesses his life and work.

Walker, Helen M. "The Contributions of Karl Pearson." *Journal of the American Statistical Association* 53 (March 1958): 11–22.
Assesses the significance of Pearson's work at the centennial of his birth.

Williams, Richard H. "On the Intellectual Versatility of Karl Pearson." *Human Nature Review* 3 (May 14, 2003): 296–301.
Describes both the remarkable range and power of Pearson's intellect and the personality flaws that had a destructive effect on the later development of research.

Web Sites

Karl Pearson: A Reader's Guide. URL: http://www.economics.soton.ac.uk/staff/aldrich/kpreader.htm. Accessed on June 12, 2006.
A large collection of links to background material on Pearson and his statistical concepts, compiled by John Aldrich of the University of Southampton, England.

Sir Francis Galton F.R.S. 1822–1911. URL: http://galton.org. Accessed on July 21, 2006.

    Presents overviews of Galton's work in statistics, genetics, psychology, and other areas.

Materials for the History of Statistics. The University of York. URL: http://www.york.ac.uk/depts/maths/histstat. Accessed on July 10, 2006.

    Offers a variety of links to biographies and background ideas in statistics and general mathematics.

3
SURMISES AND SIMULATIONS

JOHN VON NEUMANN PUTS THE COMPUTER IN PLAY

B y the 1930s, the field of mathematics had become in various ways disturbing, exciting, promising, and tumultuous. Mathematics had turned inward, in an attempt to discover its own limitations. Kurt Gödel, for example, had assigned special numbers to mathematical assertions and created a sort of algebra by which he could prove that any comprehensive mathematical system contained assertions that could not be proven using the rules of that system. Meanwhile, working independently, Alonzo Church and Alan Turing had developed the theory of computability, showing that a theoretical "universal computer" could in principle compute anything that could be computed.

Computers, indeed, were on the way. And one of the first mathematicians to design them and embrace their possibilities was John von Neumann. Von Neumann would also make significant contributions in fields as diverse as pure logic, simulation, game theory, and quantum physics.

Young Genius in a Brilliant City

John von Neumann was born on December 28, 1903, in Budapest, Hungary, to a Jewish family that had banking interests but also

John von Neumann was a multi-talented mathematician and pioneer computer scientist. Besides specifying the architecture of the modern computer, von Neumann made important contributions to quantum physics, game theory, and simulated automata. (LANL/ Photo Researchers, Inc.)

cultivated intellectual activity. (His original name was actually János Lajos Neumann.)

When he was six years old, von Neumann was already displaying genius-level performance in a number of areas. He could multiply or divide two eight-digit numbers in his head, and he evidently thought everyone else could too. According to numerous biographies, one day, when he saw his mother apparently staring off into space, von Neumann asked her, "What are you calculating?"

The boy's evident genius was not limited to mathematics. At about the same age that he was acting as a human calculating machine, von Neumann was also conversing with his classically minded father in ancient Greek. His learning was aided by his photographic memory, and his reading was prodigious—when he was eight, he began to read the family's 44-volume set of "Universal History."

Budapest was a good place for a young genius to grow up. By the turn of the 20th century, it had become a great center of science and culture. Von Neumann's biographer, Norman Macrae, suggests that the city was "about to produce one of the most glittering single generations of scientists, writers, artists, musicians, and useful expatriate millionaires to come from one small community since the city-states of the Italian Renaissance." Such a place would provide ample stimulation for a boy who often seemed to be lost in a fascinating world of numbers and logic. Young von Neumann was also fortunate in that unlike other child geniuses such as Norbert Wiener, he was not put under constant parental pressure to master every subject quickly and perfectly.

Finding a Career

In 1911, von Neumann entered the Lutheran Gymnasium, essentially an elite college preparatory school. However, even there he was soon far ahead of his fellow students and even most of his teachers, doing math at the college graduate level.

Despite the young man's prodigious talent in the field, von Neumann's father opposed his pursuing a career in pure mathematics. Therefore, when von Neumann entered the University of Berlin in 1921 and then the prestigious University of Technology in Zurich in 1923, he ended up with an undergraduate degree in chemical engineering, a field that offered secure professional employment.

At the same time, von Neumann continued to pursue his first love, mathematics. After leaving Berlin but before enrolling at Zurich, he also enrolled at Budapest University as a candidate for a doctoral degree in mathematics. Amazingly, he managed to get near-perfect grades in his chemical engineering courses while working on his mathematics thesis in set theory and passing his final exams with highest honors, earning his Ph.D. in mathematics in 1926. He then served for several years as a private lecturer (a sort of unpaid associate professor) at Berlin and the University of Hamburg.

Contributions to Physics and Mathematics

In 1930, von Neumann was invited to lecture at Princeton University in New Jersey. After his arrival in the United States, he took a post as a professor of mathematical physics at Princeton. However, he soon accepted one of the first faculty positions in Princeton's Institute for Advanced Study. For the rest of his career, von Neumann would serve in various capacities there and as a consultant for the U.S. government.

The establishment of this organization marked the beginning of the emergence of the United States as a world-class center for physics, fully competitive with the great universities and laboratories of Europe. (Many top scientific researchers, including Albert Einstein, would soon flee the growing power of Nazism in Germany.)

Since the 1920s, the physics of the atom had been a dramatic arena of scientific controversy. Competing mathematical descriptions of the behavior of atomic particles were being offered by Erwin Schrödinger's wave equations and Werner Heisenberg's matrix approach. Von Neumann showed that the two theories were mathematically equivalent. His 1932 book, *The Mathematical Foundations of Quantum Mechanics,* remains a standard textbook to this day. Von Neumann also developed a new form of algebra, where "rings of operators" could be used to describe the kind of dimensional space encountered in quantum mechanics.

Other early mathematical contributions by von Neumann included his 1925 doctoral thesis on a paradox in set theory. Bertrand Russell had proposed a famous paradox: Is the set of all sets that are not members of themselves a member of itself? Whether one says the set is a member of itself or that it is not, one ends up in a contradiction.

Von Neumann, however, showed (in two different ways) that no mathematical set could be a member of itself, offering a way out of the paradox. Von Neumann was able to further develop this idea in relation to Kurt Gödel's 1930 incompleteness theorem by suggesting that it also meant that a system of mathematical axioms could not be used to prove its own consistency.

Economics and Game Theory

Just as new, more sophisticated mathematical tools were revolutionizing physics, von Neumann developed ways to apply them to economics. In doing so, von Neumann laid the foundations for what would come to be called game theory (see chapter 4, "A Delicate Equilibrium").

In 1928, von Neumann wrote a paper on the "theory of games." He began by explaining:

> *Any event—given the external conditions and the participants in the situation (provided that the latter are acting of their own free will)—may be regarded as a game of strategy if one looks at the effect it has on the participants.*

ISSUES: VON NEUMANN AND THE BOMB

By the late 1930s, von Neumann had also become involved in military consulting, particularly with regard to the physics and design of high explosives. When the Manhattan Project (the effort to build the first nuclear bomb) came along in the early 1940s von Neumann applied his knowledge to contribute to the design of the explosive lens, in which conventional explosives were used to compress the plutonium core of the bomb in order to create an almost instantaneous critical mass and resulting nuclear explosion. Von Neumann also calculated that having bombs (conventional or nuclear) burst above the ground would maximize their destructive force. Von Neumann then made early suggestions that helped lead to the development of the hydrogen bomb. He would later be criticized, because, unlike many other nuclear scientists of the time, he never expressed regret at the development of such weapons.

The question of how much responsibility scientists have for the destructive use of their discoveries and inventions is a complex one. In a democracy, at least, it is the representatives of the people, not scientists themselves, who make the ultimate decision—but how can a public that is ignorant of science and technology make good decisions about its use? Other scientists of the time, such as Norbert Wiener, a mathematical genius comparable to von Neumann, came to quite a different conclusion. These scientists eventually refused to do military-related work and instead used their writings to try to educate the public about what they saw as the danger of technology being controlled by people who did not understand or care about its devastating consequences.

In 1954, von Neumann was appointed by President Dwight D. Eisenhower to join the Atomic Energy Commission, the body that would be in charge of controlling access to nuclear materials as well as developing a civilian nuclear power industry. In accepting the position, von Neumann did express the belief that scientists working in the nuclear field had a responsibility to help in the administration of that technology. Von Neumann also testified before Congress, urging that the government not confuse "a technical opinion [of a scientist] with a political intention" and to not remove vital security clearances from dissident scientists arbitrarily.

He considered a particular type of game or competition that was zero sum (that is, for every winner there was a loser) and in which both players knew all the possible strategies and their consequences. (In theory, this would be like a game of tic-tac-toe or, to an extent, a game of chess between two equally matched grandmasters). Von Neumann showed that, for this sort of competition, each player can find a "mini-max" strategy that is guaranteed to minimize his or her losses regardless of the strategy chosen by the opponent. There is thus an optimal strategy that would be chosen by knowledgeable, rational players.

Working together with mathematician Oskar Morgenstern, von Neumann later generalized the theory to allow for more than two players and to account for players not having complete information about possible strategies. Their 1944 book, *The Theory of Games and Economic Behavior,* essentially defined the modern field of game theory.

Need for Speed

In the late 1930s, the growing need for lengthy calculations in both science and engineering was straining the computing resources of the time, which mainly consisted of glorified adding machines staffed by battalions of workers called computers—who generally were women.

Considerable interest was therefore being shown in the design of machines that could perform calculations more quickly and that included the capability of following a complicated series of steps—a program. Alan Turing and Alonzo Church had shown that it was theoretically possible to build a universal computer that could perform any calculation that could be mathematically defined. However, it was not clear what type of technology would be practicable for such a machine.

As von Neumann worked on a variety of problems in ballistics, aerodynamics, and, later, the design of nuclear weapons, he became acquainted both with British research in calculators and the massive Harvard Mark I programmable calculator built by American engineer Howard Aiken. This latter machine used a vast number of electromechanical relays (similar to automatic telephone switches).

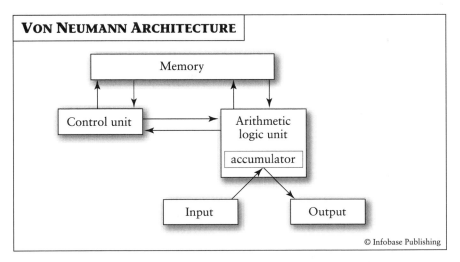

A key feature of von Neumann's architecture for the modern computer is the storing of programs in memory. This also allows programs to modify their own instructions.

A little later, von Neumann learned that two engineers at the University of Pennsylvania, J. Presper Eckert and John Mauchly, were working on a new kind of machine—an electronic digital computer called ENIAC that used vacuum tubes for its switching and memory, making it about a thousand times faster than the Mark I. Although the first version of ENIAC had already been built by the time von Neumann came on board, he served as a consultant to the project at the University of Pennsylvania's Moore School.

Designing the Digital Computer

It seemed clear that electronics rather than mechanics would be the way to go in computing, but there remained the question of how best to arrange the various parts of the machine. In particular, how were programs to be read and stored so the machine could use them to process data?

The earliest computers (such as the Mark I) read instructions from cards or tape, discarding each instruction as it was performed. This meant, for example, that to program a loop for repeating instructions, an actual loop of tape would have to be mounted and run over and over. The electronic ENIAC was too fast for tape readers to keep up, so it had to be programmed by setting thousands of switches to store instructions and constant values. This tedious procedure meant that it was not practical to use the machine for anything other than massive problems that would run for many days.

Von Neumann then contributed a key insight: The computer's working memory should not only be used to store each batch of data needed during processing; it should also be used to store the program instructions themselves. With programs in memory, looping or other decision making could be accomplished simply by "jumping" from one memory location to another.

All modern computers would therefore have two forms of memory: relatively fast memory for holding instructions and a slower form of storage that could hold large amounts of data and the results of processing. (In today's PCs, these functions are provided by the random access memory [RAM] and hard drive, respectively.)

In general, von Neumann took the hybrid electronic and mechanical design of ENIAC and conceived of a design that would be all-electronic in its internal operations and store data in the most natural form possible for an

The U.S. Army built EDVAC as the next generation of digital computer after the wartime ENIAC. Beginning operation in 1951, EDVAC embodied von Neumann's ideas about computer architecture and processing. (U.S. Army)

electronic machine—binary, with 1 and 0 representing the on-and-off switching states and, in memory, two possible marks indicated by magnetism, voltage levels, or some other phenomenon. This logical design would be consistent and largely independent of the particular type of hardware used, which would repeatedly change as computers went from vacuum tubes to transistors and integrated circuits.

In his "First Draft of a Report on the EDVAC" (1945) and his more comprehensive "Preliminary Discussion of the Logical Design of an Electronic Computing Instrument" (1946), von Neumann would establish the basic architecture and design principles of the modern electronic digital computer. They would soon be used in successive computers that featured whimsical names such as MANIAC.

Eckert and Mauchly and some of their supporters would later claim that they had already conceived of the idea of storing programs in memory, and in fact, they had already designed a form of internal memory called a mercury delay line. Whatever the truth in this assertion, the fact remains that von Neumann provided the comprehensive theoretical architecture for the modern computer, and it became known as the von Neumann architecture. Von Neumann's reports would be distributed widely and would guide the beginnings of computer science research in many parts of the world.

Looking beyond the EDVAC project, von Neumann, together with Herman Goldstine and Arthur Burks, designed a new computer for the Institute for Advanced Study (IAS) that would embody the von Neumann principles. The IAS machine's design would in turn lead to the development of research computers for the RAND Corporation, the Los Alamos National Laboratory, and in several countries, including Australia, Israel, and even the Soviet Union. The design would eventually be commercialized by IBM in the form of the IBM 701.

In his later years, von Neumann would continue to explore the theory of computing. He studied ways to design computers that could automatically maintain reliability despite the loss of certain components.

The Self-Reproducing Automaton

During the early 1950s, von Neumann began to work with the idea that a machine could be designed to interact with its environment, grow, and even reproduce. If so, von Neumann argued, one might have to call such a machine "alive." In one of his lectures, he described the machine in terms of a robot consisting of a small number of standardized parts:

> *I will introduce as elementary units neurons, a "muscle," entities which make and cut fixed contacts, and entities which supply energy, all defined with about that degree of superficiality with which [the theory of neural networks] describes an actual neuron. If you describe muscles, connective tissues, "disconnecting tissues," and means of providing metabolic energy . . . you probably wind up with something like 10 or 12 or 15 elementary parts.*

Von Neumann then went on to ask:

> *Can one build an aggregate out of such elements in such a manner that if it is put into a reservoir, in which there float all these elements in large numbers, it will then begin to construct other aggregates, each of which will at the end turn out to be another automaton exactly like the original one?*

Von Neumann decided that it would not be possible to build a real, functioning machine with the available technology. Instead, he designed a sort of virtual machine showing the kind of logic a machine might use to carry out its life processes. As he worked on it, the design grew more and more complicated. It became difficult to keep track of the activities of the machine's hundreds of separate parts.

Meanwhile, another great mathematician, Stanisław Ulam, had been doing pioneering work in computer simulations. Ulam programmed sets of rules that the computer could use to draw patterns on a grid of squares. The patterns often turned out to be surprisingly complex and beautiful (one set of rules produced a delicate, coral-like growth from a single square).

Ulam worked with von Neumann to translate his "living machine" concepts into a set of rules that could be used to manipulate patterns on the computer. Ulam and von Neumann hoped that one day they

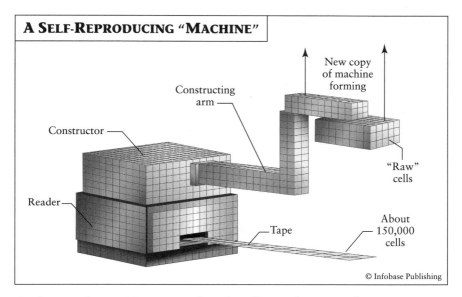

A SELF-REPRODUCING "MACHINE"

A schematic for von Neumann's idea of a self-reproducing machine. It assumes that the machine receives its instructions by interacting with data on a very long tape. Following precise rules, the machine gradually builds a copy of itself from data cells in the simulated environment.

could at least simulate a "living machine" in the computer, leaving the actual construction of the machine to a future generation.

Ulam put von Neumann's machine into a "world" that consisted of an endless grid of squares that he called cells. The cells would behave according to a set of rules that would determine their new state according to the conditions of their surrounding cells. For example, a cell that was surrounded by enough "food" cells might change from one state, where the cell is surviving but not growing, to another state, where one of its neighbors is added to the growing "organism."

Von Neumann further refined Ulam's work. His final design for the "living" automaton was very complex. There were 200,000 cells that, like the cells in the human body, had different specialties (such as copying information, growing, or reproducing). Cells could have any one of 29 possible states—represented by different colors. Because of its use of many individual cells governed by automatic rules, the simulated organism became known as a cellular automaton.

Although von Neumann was able to prove mathematically that such an automaton would work (if the parts could actually be made), his health failed before he could develop the ideas further. However later researchers would develop many other types of cellular automata (see chapter 7, "Games of Emergence" and chapter 10, "A New Kind of Science?").

A Difficult Fate

In many ways, John von Neumann was larger than life. In addition to his bold intellectual speculations and his dominating presence in academic politics, he enjoyed food, drink, and attending parties where ribald commentary was the order of the day. On February 8, 1957, however, von Neumann died of bone cancer, which had become excruciatingly painful and had spread to his brain. Von Neumann seems to have undergone a psychological and spiritual crisis in his last days as he faced death (which he viewed as an end to the exquisite possibilities of thought) and as he was robbed of the intellect that he had so highly prized.

Von Neumann received many awards reflecting his diverse contributions to American science and technology. These include the Distinguished Civilian Service Award (1947), the Presidential Medal of Freedom (1956), and the Enrico Fermi Award (1956).

To some critics of cold-war nuclear policy, von Neumann was at least a partial accomplice in the unleashing of the nuclear demon. However, mathematicians and physicists continue to turn to him as an example of creative, original ideas. For computer scientists, von Neumann was perhaps the person who did the most to shape the design of the marvelous machines that sit today on so many desktops—and to introduce the computer as a universal tool for simulation.

Chronology

1903   John von Neumann is born on December 28 in Budapest, Hungary

OTHER SCIENTISTS: STANISŁAW ULAM

Stanisław Ulam (1909–84) was a Polish-American mathematician who was invited by John von Neumann to join him in the secret nuclear bomb project during World War II. There Ulam developed a key type of computer simulation that relied upon repeated generation of random numbers to mimic the distribution generated by natural laws. (Because of its use of chance, the method was named Monte Carlo after the famous casino resort.)

Ulam contributed to a variety of other aspects of mathematics, including set theory and topology. As his career advanced, Ulam moved away from detailed mathematical work to posing problems and possible connections between mathematical concepts and phenomena in physics and biology.

In a tribute to von Neumann, Ulam recalled that they had a conversation in which they discussed ". . . the ever accelerating progress of technology and changes in the mode of human life, which gives the appearance of approaching some essential singularity in the history of the race beyond which human affairs, as we know them, could not continue." This idea would be further explored starting in the 1990s by science fiction writer Vernor Vinge and inventor and artificial intelligence theorist Ray Kurzweil.

1911	Von Neumann enters high school but is soon doing college-level mathematics
1921	Von Neumann attends the University of Berlin to study chemical engineering
1923	Von Neumann moves to the University of Technology in Zurich and earns an undergraduate degree in chemical engineering
1926	Having periodically returned to Hungary to pursue his mathematics studies, von Neumann earns his doctorate in mathematics at the University of Budapest
1926–30	Von Neumann serves as a lecturer in Berlin and Hamburg
1931	Von Neumann becomes a professor of mathematical physics at Princeton University

1944	Von Neumann and Oskar Morgenstern publish *The Theory of Games and Economic Behavior*
1945	Von Neumann's draft report on the EDVAC begins his design for the architecture of modern electronic digital computing
1948	Von Neumann begins his work on cellular automata
1954	Von Neumann is appointed to the United States Atomic Energy Commission
1957	Von Neumann dies on February 8 of bone cancer

Further Reading

Books

Aspray, William. *John von Neumann and the Origins of Modern Computing.* Cambridge, Mass.: MIT Press, 1990.
> Describes the key ideas that von Neumann contributed to the architecture that is found in nearly all computers today.

Heims, S. J. *John von Neumann and Norbert Wiener: From Mathematics to the Technologies of Life and Death.* Cambridge, Mass.: MIT Press, 1980.
> A study of how two geniuses were influenced by (and in turn dealt with) the implications of technology at the service of the military-industrial complex.

MacRae, Norman. *John von Neumann: The Scientific Genius Who Pioneered the Modern Computer, Game Theory, Nuclear Deterrence, and Much More.* 2nd ed. Providence, R.I.: American Mathematical Society, 1999.
> A readable, detailed modern biography of von Neumann that includes previously unpublished information from interviews with colleagues.

von Neumann, John. *The Computer and the Brain.* New Haven, Conn.: Yale University Press, 1958.
> Includes some of von Neumann's predictions about the future development of computers.

———. *Theory of Self-Reproducing Automata.* Urbana: University of Illinois Press, 1966.
> Collection of papers containing the first key developments in the theory of cellular automata.

Articles

Lee, J. A. N. "John Louis von Neumann" Available online. URL: http://ei.cs.vt.edu/~history/VonNeumann.html. Accessed on July 3, 2006.

> Biographical sketch focusing on von Neumann's contributions to computer design.

Ulam, Stanisław. "Tribute to John von Neumann." *Bulletin of the American Mathematical Society* 64 (May 1958): 1–49.

4

A DELICATE
EQUILIBRIUM

JOHN NASH AND GAME THEORY

During the 1970s, Princeton students would sometimes enter their classrooms in the morning to find that someone had filled the blackboard with a mysterious mixture of abstruse mathematical formulas and unknown codes. According to campus lore, there was a phantom who roamed the halls at night, sometimes shoving papers filled with numerological calculations under a professor's office door.

Unknown to the students (and even most of the faculty), the phantom was a mathematician named John Forbes Nash. Two decades earlier, Nash had revolutionized the understanding of how players in a game—or participants in a business transaction or a labor conflict—formulate strategies and reach a particular result. This "game theory" was now revolutionizing economics, but its originator was lost in a world of delusion, painfully groping for a way back to the life he had known as one of the world's great mathematical thinkers.

A "Different" Child

John Nash was born on June 13, 1928, in the Appalachian town of Bluefield, West Virginia. His father (of the same name) was an electrical engineer who worked for the local utility company, and his mother, Margaret, had been a schoolteacher. Both parents were intelligent, disciplined, and energetic.

As Nash noted in his Nobel Prize autobiography, "Bluefield, a small city in a comparatively remote geographical location in the Appalachians, was not a community of scholars or of high technology." However, the town had become an important regional business center.

The local schools could be described as sound but limited in their curricula. Young Nash, however, did have access in his parents' and grandparents' homes to a good encyclopedia and some other books of interest. He was also tutored by his mother, an experienced teacher who took a lively interest in his education all the way through high school. That interest was shared by Nash's father, who answered his numerous questions but also handed him science books.

John Forbes Nash blazed like a meteor in the mathematical sky of the 1950s, particularly in his discovery of the Nash equilibrium in game theory. Nash then descended into a decades-long struggle with schizophrenia, gradually emerging and sharing the Nobel Prize in economics in 1994. (Photo by Fred Prouser, © Reuters/CORBIS)

In school, however, young Nash was socially awkward and tended to ignore the rules, regularly earning bad marks for deportment. He could not wait to go home, where he had turned his room into a laboratory. He tinkered with radios and other electrical gadgets and did chemistry experiments. The latter eventually became rather dangerous, as he and two other boys turned to making and detonating various sorts of explosives.

Nash later recalled in the PBS documentary *A Brilliant Madness* that

One time, somebody suggested that I was a prodigy. Another time it was suggested that I should be called "bug brains" because I had ideas, but they were sort of buggy or not perfectly sound.

Nash's parents tried to make him well rounded by enrolling him in activities such as Boy Scout camp, Sunday Bible classes, a dancing school, and a youth club. They even enlisted Nash's younger sister to try to get him involved with after-school social activities. Nash did not openly rebel against being forced to participate in these activities, but he endured them until he could return to his lab.

When classmates made fun of the tall but awkward boy, he responded by demonstrating his intellectual superiority and, sometimes, by playing nasty practical jokes involving electricity. Years later, many of Nash's colleagues would encounter the same mixture of awkwardness and arrogance.

A Wayward Path to Math

In high school, Nash was intrigued by reading *Men of Mathematics,* a classic set of biographies by E. T. Bell that romanticized the world of mathematics. Nash's parents arranged for him to receive some mathematics courses at nearby Bluefield College, but he still envisioned following his father into a career in electrical engineering. In his senior year, Nash won a Westinghouse scholarship, one of only 10 awarded each year.

When he enrolled for college at the Carnegie Institute of Technology (later Carnegie-Mellon University) in Pittsburgh, Nash decided to major in chemical engineering. Gradually becoming frustrated with the tedium of laboratory work (and his awkwardness with delicate instruments), Nash eventually switched his major to mathematics at the urging of faculty members who had observed his talent in that area. By the time he graduated, he had earned so much credit in mathematics that he was awarded a master's degree along with his bachelor's.

Nash's excellent record brought him offers of graduate fellowships from both Harvard and Princeton. Nash decided on the latter because it offered more generous terms and because Princeton was closer to the family home in Bluefield.

Life at Princeton

Nash stood out sharply from the other students, often in uncomfortable ways. Mel Hausner, a colleague from Nash's Princeton days, recounts in the documentary *A Brilliant Madness* that

> *when John walked into the room you knew that John walked into the room. I think he thought of himself as superior, intellectually, mathematically superior. We thought highly of ourselves and each other, but with John it was double. John was just very clearly above it.*

Nash frequently cut classes, claiming that what really counted was original work. He deliberately avoided learning what other people were doing about a particular problem. And he wanted to tackle only the toughest problems, the ones that had defeated the best mathematicians.

On the other hand, Nash's undeniable brilliance and imagination greatly impressed many of the students. Games were very popular among the Princeton mathematics students. They played chess, Kriegspiel (a variant form of chess with hidden pieces), and an Asian strategy game called Go that was very popular.

Shortly after Nash's arrival at Princeton, he invented and introduced a strategy game that came to be called Nash. The game was played on a rhombus-shaped board of hexagons with pairs of black and white sides, with the winner being the first player to play a row of stones from one of his sides to the other. (It turned out later that a Danish person named Piet Hein had independently invented the game a few years earlier and later marketed it under the name Hex.) Nash proved mathematically that on any size board the player with the first move could always win.

Game Theory and the Nash Equilibrium

Nash's interest in games soon grew much deeper than indulging in an hour's pastime over a board. The biggest games of all went by the names economics, the market, trade negotiations, and so on. Nash's interest in economics had begun with a course he took as an undergraduate at Carnegie. Frustratingly, though, advanced mathematicians had given little attention to the problems of economics. One exception, though, was the work of John von Neumann and Oskar Morgenstern on game theory (see chapter 3, "Surmises and Simulations").

By the time Nash arrived there, von Neumann dominated the Princeton scene, having done dazzling work in areas ranging from math to physics to designing nuclear weapons to economic analysis. After Nash attended one of von Neumann's lectures, he quickly became hooked on game theory and its variety of possible applications to virtually every field of human endeavor. He also saw that von Neumann and Morgenstern's work, though impressive, was far from complete. It had left many unanswered questions about the very kind of "games" that mattered to economists: markets with many players, imperfect knowledge, and no tidy "zero sum" solution.

GAME PAYOFF MATRIX

		Player 2 Confess	Refuse
Player 1	Confess	2,2	4,0
	Refuse	0,4	3,3

© Infobase Publishing

A payoff matrix in game theory shows the resulting score for each player based on the moves chosen by each. Here the matrix represents a version of the well-known game Prisoner's Dilemma. The Nash equilibrium for this game occurs when both players confess, giving each a sentence of two years.

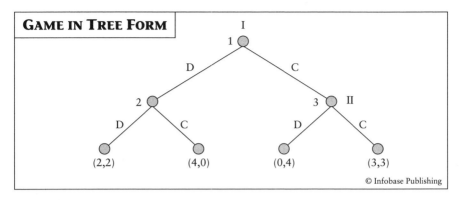

GAME IN TREE FORM

© Infobase Publishing

"Extensive form" is another way to diagram games in game theory. This treelike structure branches out for the possible combinations of moves by each player. (This diagram uses the same version of the Prisoner's Dilemma as the preceding figure did.)

Zero sum games were relatively easy to describe because there was normally a winner and a loser. Nash wanted to consider games with more than two players and in which there were moves or strategies that were better or worse—but not necessarily producing a clear winner.

In his first game theory paper, "The Bargaining Problem," Nash looked at transactions, the fundamental basis of economics, where people make agreements to exchange money, goods, or services. Nash said the essential feature of bargaining is that "two individuals [have] the opportunity to collaborate for mutual benefit in more than one way." The individuals may have different goals and expectations, and they will each offer terms to the other based on them. To be successful, both sides' final demands have to be met from the total amount of "utility" (such as money or goods) available.

Instead of starting with axioms and trying to derive a solution (the most common approach in traditional mathematics), Nash turned the process around. He defined the conditions that had to be satisfied by a successful bargain, formalized them mathematically, and then showed that there was a unique solution that maximized the utility value to both bargainers.

In the more general language of games, Nash showed that in a game each player will have a particular strategy that best counters the strategies chosen by all the other players. At this point, the game can be said to have reached equilibrium—now called a Nash equilibrium. Nash's mathematical proof that such an equilibrium must exist revolutionized game theory and made it suddenly applicable to many real-world economic situations.

However, it would take many years before most economists realized the power of the tools they had been given. In part this was because not all mathematicians were interested in Nash's work in game theory, unlike his world-class proofs in algebraic geometry and differential equations. But in part the delay would come because in a few years Nash himself would virtually disappear from the mathematical scene.

Falling Short

Nash secured a position as an instructor at the Massachusetts Institute of Technology (MIT), but his abrasive personality worked against him. Besides having difficult relations with colleagues, Nash also had difficulty with intimate relationships. He met and dated a nurse named Eleanor Stier. When he discovered that she was pregnant with their child, Nash refused to support the baby or even pay for its delivery. Nash kept the affair secret, and his son John would grow up without any contact with his father for many years.

Nash then became involved with 21-year-old Alicia Lopez-Harrison de Lardé, a physics major and one of Nash's students. Alicia was attractive, exotic, and interested in a serious scientific career of her own. Nash and Lardé were married in February 1957.

As 1958 began, Nash seemed to be at the top of the world. *Fortune* magazine listed him as one of the brightest stars in the current mathematical firmament, and he had a wife who shared many of his interests. But Nash had just turned 30, and as biographer Sylvia Nasar noted, "For a mathematician turning 30 is a lot like for a ballet dancer or an athlete. Age is your enemy."

Always setting the highest hurdles for his race with himself, Nash decided that he had fallen short. After a decade of brilliant work, he had failed to win the prestigious Fields medal, pretty much the closest thing

---

I WAS THERE: INFURIATING BUT SO BRILLIANT

When biographers and interviewers asked Nash's MIT colleagues to recount their experiences with him, a number of adjectives kept popping up. In *A Brilliant Madness,* Felix Browder calls Nash "[an] out and out and uninhibited and shameless elitist." Zipporah Levinson says that Nash "was very brash, very boastful, very selfish, very egocentric. His colleagues did not like him especially, but they tolerated him because his mathematics were so brilliant."

Indeed, Nash was viewed with awe. Donald Newman recalled that

I was thinking about a problem, trying to get somewhere with it, and I couldn't and I couldn't and I couldn't. And I went to sleep one night and I dreamt. I did not dream directly of the solution to that problem. Rather, I dreamt that I met Nash and I asked him the problem, and he told me the answer. When I did finally write the paper, I gave him credit. It was not my solution; I could not have done it myself.

---

mathematics had to a Nobel Prize. He tried to redouble his efforts by seeking to prove the Riemann Hypothesis, a fiendishly difficult conjecture about complex and prime numbers that remains unproven today.

Breakdown

Although a solution sometimes seemed tantalizingly close, Nash failed to prove the Riemann Hypothesis. His efforts left him physically exhausted and mentally depressed. Such conditions can precipitate a psychotic breakdown in a person who has certain underlying mental conditions such as schizophrenia.

On New Year's Eve 1958, Nash went to a costume party at the home of a colleague. He dressed as a baby, wearing a diaper. Although the baby is a traditional symbol of the New Year, Nash's actual behavior seemed even more eccentric and disturbing than usual. A few weeks later, Nash went into the MIT common room and announced that space aliens were sending him coded messages via the *New York Times*. The strange declarations continued: Nash said that he was on the cover of *Life* magazine, disguised as Pope John XXIII—23 being his favorite prime number. Nash then noticed that there were many men on the MIT campus who were wearing red ties—they must be part of a communist conspiracy! The strange ideas seemed to come one after another, without seeming connection. One time Nash turned down a prestigious position offered by the University of Chicago because, as he explained, he was already scheduled to become emperor of Antarctica.

The head of the math department, hoping that Nash was only having a temporary nervous breakdown, gave him a month off from teaching. Nash drove to Washington, D.C., and tried to deliver letters to various foreign governments by dropping them into embassy mail slots. Increasingly worried and even desperate, Alicia consulted with psychiatrists who advised that Nash be hospitalized.

Nash was taken against his will to McClean Hospital, a private psychiatric facility outside of Boston. The doctors there diagnosed Nash as a paranoid schizophrenic, sedated him, and put him into psychoanalysis.

Schizophrenia is a mental disorder whose cause is uncertain (although many researchers suspect an organic or biochemical origin). Even today, treatment and management of the condition is difficult, although a variety of medications can help control symptoms. Some patients gradually improve or even completely recover.

In the Shadowlands

After 50 days, Nash was able to secure his release from the hospital. He went to Europe, eventually leaving Alicia and embarking on a surrealistic journey where he tried to dodge supposed communist and anticommunist plotters. After nine months, American embassy officials were able to have Nash deported and returned to the United States.

Nash's condition failed to improve. The next time he was hospitalized, it was in Trenton State Hospital in New Jersey, where conditions were much less comfortable than they had been at the private facility. Doctors there treated Nash with insulin shock therapy, a controversial attempt to "reset" the metabolic foundation of the brain that had already been abandoned by many hospitals by that time.

CONNECTIONS: MATH AND MADNESS?

It has long been a common belief that people who engage in high-level intellectual work are at higher risk of mental illness. The 17th-century poet John Dryden put it this way in his poem *Absalom and Achitophel*

> *Great wits are sure to madness near allied,*
> *And thin partitions do their bounds divide.*

Anecdotally, some evidence for this assertion is reflected in stories of two world chess champions, Paul Morphy and Wilhelm Steinitz, who ended their careers in the mental asylum, not to mention the erratic trajectory of Bobby Fischer. Of course, popular culture has contributed the stereotypical image of the cackling mad scientist—perhaps the closest real-life example being the electrical wizard Nikola Tesla.

Among mathematicians, perhaps the best known for psychological problems is Georg Cantor, the German mathematician who pioneered set theory and showed that there was more than one kind of infinity. Cantor suffered from recurring bouts of depression in his later years. But while a number of mathematicians (such as Paul Erdos) are known for their eccentricity, there seems to be little evidence that mathematicians are more prone to madness than other types of intellectuals.

A recent study by Connie M. Strong and Terence A. Ketter of Stanford University suggests that one particular form of mental illness called bipolar disorder (which is characterized by extreme mood swings) may involve certain traits such as openness and imaginativeness that are also shared by creative people such as the best mathematicians.

John Nash, however, suffered from schizophrenia, a different condition. Nash's mathematical skill seemed to both serve and betray him in his battle with his illness. On the one hand, his skill may have initially strengthened his sense of identity and mental coherence, staving off his first schizophrenic break. When Nash did have a breakdown and suffered delusions, however, mathematics, in the form of numerology, served to buttress his elaborate conspiracy theories. Finally, though, Nash turned his mathematical logic against his delusions, apparently weaning himself from them by revealing their inconsistencies.

Again, the pattern of seeming improvement was followed by a new bout of delusion. Feeling she could no longer cope with Nash's condition, Alicia filed for divorce in 1962.

The Long Climb Back

Nash's colleagues at Princeton and MIT did not abandon him. They tried to keep him stable, with an apartment, regular visits to a psychiatrist (who prescribed one of the first antipsychotic medications), and an academic position that had only light duties. Again, however, Nash kept slipping back into the world of delusion. In 1970, Alicia decided to return to Nash's life—not as a wife, but as a friend who could give him the constant help he seemed to need.

As the Nash equilibrium emerged as a central idea for understanding economic transactions and negotiations ranging from business mergers to auctions to collective bargaining, many economists wondered why game theory was not turning up in any of the annual Nobel Prizes in their field. What they did not realize was that the Nobel Prize committee in Stockholm, Sweden, did not think any prize could be given for game theory without including John Nash for his key role in the development of the field. However, the committee also believed that such a psychologically unstable person as Nash could not hold up under the publicity and stress that the prize would inevitably bring.

But things were slowly changing for John Nash. He had begun to systematically question the hallucinatory voices in his head, applying something like the rigor of mathematical inquiry to their claims. He began to reject the voices. The voices did not necessarily go away, but he was refusing to listen to them. As Nash says in *A Brilliant Madness,* "I willed it. I decided I was going to think rationally."

Nash began to reconnect to the world and his colleagues. While they assumed that he was taking some new, more effective medication, Nash had actually stopped taking medication in 1970.

Nobel Triumph

As the 1990s began and word of Nash's recovery was spreading, the Nobel committee made its decision. On December 10, 1994,

Nash, now 66 years old, received the Nobel Prize in economics in Stockholm, sharing it with two other game theoreticians.

In 2001, Nash and Alicia were remarried. Today Nash has returned to MIT to work in mathematics. That same year, the film *A Beautiful Mind,* loosely based on Sylvia Nasar's 1998 biography of Nash, introduced the mathematician's strange life and poignant struggle to the general public. Although the film movingly portrayed Nash's battle with mental illness, it oversimplified or omitted many details and had difficulty conveying the nature and significance of Nash's work.

In his Nobel autobiography, Nash seems to suggest that some aspect of his creativity might have been left behind along with his madness:

> *At the present time I seem to be thinking again in the style that is characteristic of scientists. However this is not entirely a matter of joy as if someone returned from physical disability to good physical health. One aspect of this is that rationality of thought imposes a limit on a person's concept of his relation to the cosmos.*

Nash also acknowledged that, being 66 years old (at the time), it was perhaps unlikely that he would be able to add another major mathematical discovery to his achievements. Still, he suggested that perhaps the decades of "partially deluded thinking" might have provided a sort of vacation for his brain.

In recent years, Nash has undertaken a project to develop computer programs to perform calculations based on his work in game theory. One of the tools he is using is Steven Wolfram's program Mathematica (see chapter 10, "A New Kind of Science").

Regardless of what the future might bring for Nash, his legacy is secure. Nash's work, by revealing the dynamics of competition, has also given negotiators and even rivals the ability to find the best solution—the equilibrium where each player can feel that he or she has gotten the best practicable result. And Nash's struggle to restore his own inner equilibrium represents an inspiring victory over the destructive forces of irrationality.

Chronology

1928	John Forbes Nash is born on June 13 in Bluefield, West Virginia
1940	The brilliant but socially awkward young Nash performs scientific experiments in his room at home
1948	Nash receives simultaneous bachelor's and master's degrees from the Carnegie Institute of Technology
1950	Nash earns his Ph.D. in mathematics at Princeton University and joins the MIT faculty
	Nash's doctoral dissertation on noncooperative games introduces what will be called the Nash equilibrium; he develops further work on game theory in his paper "The Bargaining Problem"
1952	Nash makes a significant contribution to algebraic geometry with his paper "Real Algebraic Manifolds"
1953	Nash publishes his paper "Two-Person Cooperative Games"
1957	Nash marries Alicia Lopez-Harrison de Lardé, a physics student from El Salvador
1959	Nash is admitted to a mental hospital and is diagnosed with paranoid schizophrenia
1960s	Nash undergoes periodic psychiatric treatments, including insulin shock therapy
	Nash becomes "the phantom of Fine Hall" at Princeton, writing complex equations on classroom blackboards at night
1970s	Nash begins to emerge from mental illness, working on computer programs at Princeton and making contacts
1980s	Late in the decade, Nash begins to do new original mathematical work
	Some mathematicians begin to lobby the Nobel Prize committee to recognize Nash's work

| **1994** | Nash receives the Nobel Prize in economics |
| **2001** | Nash and Alicia remarry; the film version of *A Beautiful Mind* popularizes Nash's story of recovery from mental illness |

Further Reading

Books

Nasar, Sylvia. *A Beautiful Mind*. New York: Simon & Schuster, 1998.
> A vivid and moving biography of John Nash, including many anecdotes and recollections of colleagues.

Nash, John. *The Essential John Nash*. Princeton, N.J.: Princeton University Press, 2002.
> Contains Nash's Nobel Prize autobiography and his most important papers, as well as a description of his game of "Nash" (Hex) and an afterword.

Articles

Nash, John F. "John F. Nash, Jr.: Autobiography." Nobelprize. org. Available online. URL: http://nobelprize.org/nobel_prizes/ economics/laureates/1994/nash-autobio.html. Accessed on July 15, 2006.
> Official autobiography by Nash for his 1994 Nobel Prize in economics.

Web Sites

"A Beautiful Mind." URL: http://www.abeautifulmind.com. Accessed on June 10, 2006.
> The Web site for the Hollywood film on Nash's life starring Russell Crow and directed by Ron Howard. Includes background materials and interactive activities.

"A Brilliant Madness." PBS. URL: http://www.pbs.org/wgbh/amex/ nash. Accessed on July 16, 2006.
> Web site for a PBS documentary that conveys a more accurate account of Nash's life than is found in the movie *A Beautiful Mind*.

5

ENDLESS STRUCTURE

BENOÎT MANDELBROT OPENS THE FRACTAL PORTAL

The remarkable story of a new kind of geometry begins with a deceptively simple question: How long is the coastline of England? Get a map, note the scale, and try to get an approximate measurement with a ruler. Get a map with a smaller scale, try again, and get a still larger number. Fly along the coast and do a photographic aerial survey, and the ins and outs of shoals and shores become even longer. Finally, go to the beach and start measuring at a human scale.

It turns out that whether it is England or California, coastlines are just one of many things that have a peculiar property. There is no end to the levels of detail as one zooms in. The length of a coastline turns out to be infinite, at least until one gets down to the atomic level.

The mathematics that describes such infinitely detailed objects is called fractal geometry. In discovering this new geometry, with its endless layers of similar but unique patterns, Benoît Mandelbrot found the hidden order inside the seeming chaos of nature.

Learning in the Shadow of War

Benoît Mandelbrot was born in Warsaw, Poland, on November 20, 1924. His family was Jewish and had originally come from Lithuania. They were well educated; Mandelbrot's father was a clothing manufacturer, and his mother had been a physician.

The boy was taught at home for his first years because his mother was afraid of epidemics. He quickly mastered reading and also showed himself to be a strong chess player, winning the championship for his age group.

In 1936, when young Mandelbrot was 12 years old and Hitler was beginning to threaten Europe, the family moved to Paris. The boy's uncle Szolem Mandelbrojt taught mathematics as a university professor, and the youngster thus met many mathematicians and heard plenty of mathematical talk. Young Mandelbrot became especially interested in geometry. His uncle, who worked in advanced analysis (calculus), did not approve of this interest. He shared the opinion of many mathematicians of the time that geometry had reached a dead end and was suitable only for beginning students.

Benoît Mandelbrot is shown against a background of fractals, the endlessly unfolding structures that he made famous. (Hank Morgan/Photo Researchers, Inc.)

In September 1939, Germany started World War II by invading Poland. The next spring the Germans invaded and quickly occupied much of France, including Paris. The Mandelbrot family moved into the French countryside and had to move again frequently to avoid the Nazi police. It was thus impossible for Mandelbrot to attend any sort of regular school. As he recalled in an interview in *Mathematical People,*

> For awhile, I was moving around with a younger brother, toting around a few obsolete books and learning things my way, guessing a number of things myself, doing nothing in any rational or even half-reasonable way, and acquiring a great deal of independence and self-confidence.

Young Mandelbrot was aided in his self-directed study by his memory for shapes and his ability to recognize patterns. He later noted that

> *Faced with some complicated integral [in calculus], I instantly related it to a familiar shape ... I knew an army of shapes that I'd encountered once in some book or some problem, and remembered forever with their properties and their peculiarities.*

A Different Mathematical Path

When Paris was liberated in 1944, Mandelbrot took the national university entrance examinations. Although he had never formally studied advanced algebra or calculus, Mandelbrot found that his familiarity with geometry and facilities with shapes helped him translate problems in other kinds of mathematics into familiar forms.

In 1945, Mandelbrot's Uncle Szolem returned from the United States, where he had been living during the war. They argued about the young man's future career. Szolem supported a mathematical movement called Bourbaki, which stressed a style of mathematical analysis that was formal, strict, and elegant. Young Mandelbrot resisted his uncle's suggestions. Perhaps because his youth had been spent in a world of constant change and uncertainty, he instinctively sought a field that would have rough edges and complex texture—a world of changing geometric shapes.

Mandelbrot briefly attended the École Normale of Paris but left because they had little interest in geometry. However, at the Polytechnique School of Paris, Mandelbrot found a mathematician who shared this spirit of adventure: Paul Pierre Lévy. Lévy had become an expert in probability theory and had also studied physical phenomena that involved probability, such as the jittery random way in which small particles move in response to heat energy. Lévy helped Mandelbrot learn to look for mathematical phenomena in nature rather than only in the neat, tidy abstractions favored by many established mathematicians. Mandelbrot also took advantage of the cultural atmosphere to read widely in many different subjects and to listen to classical music.

Mandelbrot's career took a brief turn toward practicality. He went to the California Institute of Technology (Caltech) in Pasadena and earned master's and professional degrees in aeronautical engineering. Returning to France, he joined the French air force for a year, then returned to academic studies in Paris.

In 1952, Mandelbrot received his Ph.D. from the University of Paris. His doctoral thesis, "Mathematical Theories of Games of Communication," brought together ideas from thermodynamics, cybernetics (the science of communication and control pioneered by Norbert Wiener), and the game theory of John von Neumann. Mandelbrot said later that the thesis was poorly written and badly organized, but it included an idea that would be very important in his later work—structures that replicated themselves over and over again on smaller and smaller scales, such as a tree with a trunk, branches, and twigs.

During 1953 and 1954, Mandelbrot continued his mathematical explorations by being sponsored by John von Neumann for a fellowship at the Institute for Advanced Studies at Princeton, the home of many of Europe's "mathematical refugees." There he first encountered another key idea that would greatly figure in his later work: the so-called Hausdorff-Besicovitch dimension, where a sort of mathematical perspective reveals two-dimensional motion around a one-dimensional line. (The particular example he studied was the tiny but frenetic Brownian motion of molecules in a fluid.) In 1955, Mandelbrot returned to Europe, teaching in Geneva, Switzerland, and Lille, France.

Mysterious Clumps

The work that would finally bring together all of Mandelbrot's interests began in 1958, when he accepted an open-ended position in the research department of IBM. IBM was becoming the leader of the computer industry, and it, like Bell Telephone, had a policy of giving selected cutting-edge scientists some money and a laboratory and turning them loose to pursue their interests. Although the work they funded often had no immediate or direct connection with computers or telephones, such research often ended up resulting in important technical advances.

In 1961, IBM asked Mandelbrot to analyze mysterious noise that was causing problems in telephone circuits. IBM thought that the noise might be caused by workmen's tools as they made repairs to the system. However, Mandelbrot realized that the noise had a peculiar structure similar to the paths of Brownian motion. There were big bursts of noise that when analyzed more closely proved to consist of a clump of smaller bursts. The noise was inherent in the structure of the circuits themselves. Based on Mandelbrot's work, IBM canceled an expensive but futile antinoise project.

Meanwhile, Mandelbrot had turned to studying "noise" or seemingly random values in other types of data. Although he had no background in the field, Mandelbrot realized that economics is a good source of random data because there were often records of prices that went back hundreds of years. Most economists believed that the price of a commodity (such as cotton) usually moved in two ways. One kind of move had some reasonable cause, such as bad weather reducing the amount of the product available and increasing the price. The other kind of movement seemed to be erratic or random—the prices "jiggled" up and down by small amounts from hour to hour or day to day.

Economists had assumed that if the random price fluctuations were plotted on a graph, they would form the well-known bell curve pattern (see chapter 2, "Tools for Pattern-Finders"). When a class is graded on a curve, there are only a few As and Fs, more Bs and Ds, and the largest group of grades are Cs. The curve bulges in the middle at C and tapers off as you move toward the F or A ends. In other words, Mandelbrot expected that most prices would hover near the average value.

Mandelbrot had been invited by Hendrick Houthakker, a Harvard economics professor, to give a talk to his students. When Mandelbrot arrived at Houthakker's office, the graph he saw on the blackboard there looked strangely familiar. Mandelbrot had been graphing the distribution of incomes in a group of people. He had been finding that the incomes did not fall neatly into a bell curve. They tended to make a longer, flatter curve with clumps of incomes

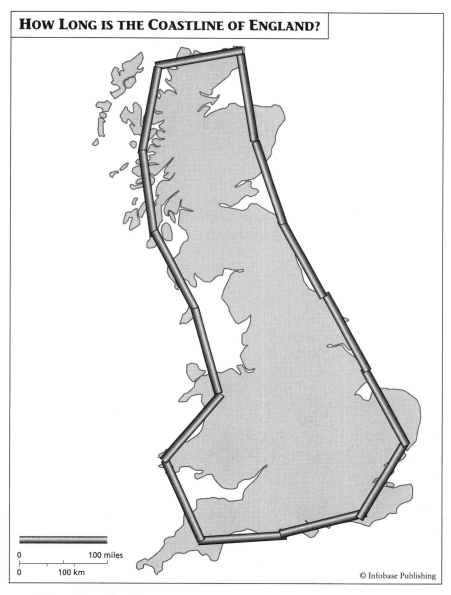

HOW LONG IS THE COASTLINE OF ENGLAND?

0   100 miles
0   100 km

© Infobase Publishing

Mandelbrot began his famous paper on fractals by asking, "How long is the coastline of England?" The map shows a first approximation developed by placing sticks of a fixed length along the edges. However, any region of the coast can be "blown up" and remeasured. Mandelbrot showed that coastlines are fractal structures that are actually infinitely long!

scattered throughout. Houthakker's graph looked very similar—
although it turned out to represent not incomes but cotton prices.

Chaos and Fractals

Mandelbrot later recalled in the interview in *Mathematical People*
that he

> *had identified a new phenomenon present in many aspects of nature,
> but all the examples were peripheral in their fields, and the phenom-
> enon itself had eluded definition. The usual term now is the Greek
> chaos, but I had been using the weaker-sounding Latin term erratic
> behavior at the time.*

(See chapter 6, "The Richness of the Random," for a different path
to this discovery.)

The erratic behavior that had showed up in incomes and cotton
prices had also appeared in physics in Brownian motion and other
forms of behavior of fluids and gases—and in Mandelbrot's earlier
work with the telephone circuits. In geometry, it showed up in patterns that were made of tiny clumps that were distributed seemingly
randomly. The patterns lacked the neatness of the straight lines and
smooth curves of Euclidean geometry, but the patterns were self-simi-
lar, that is, if one magnified the pattern, each part looked like a min-
iature copy of the whole. This could be done indefinitely, moving to a
smaller and smaller scale. Mandelbrot used the word *fractal* (meaning fractured or broken up) to describe these geometric patterns.

The Mandelbrot Set

In the 1960s, computers had just begun the transition from vacuum
tubes to the solid-state world of the transistor. Computer time was
still an expensive commodity, and Mandelbrot and his assistants
had to spend many weeks calculating fractal patterns that can now
be generated in a few seconds on a modern desktop computer.

The most intricate and beautiful discovery of Mandelbrot's research was the object that came to be known as the Mandelbrot set. The first hints had been sketched by hand years earlier, based on the work of two early 20th-century French mathematicians: Gaston Julia and

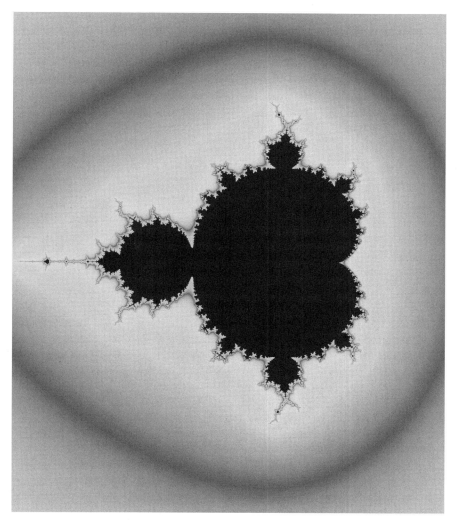

This Mandelbrot set was generated using the program Fractint for Windows. A variety of software packages (many free) allow for generating and exploring fractals.

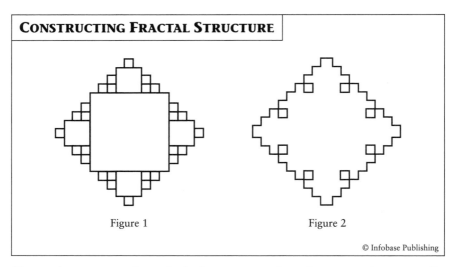

Shown above is a simple method of constructing fractal structures by repeatedly creating rectangles each a third the size of the previous level. In figure 2, the inner rectangles have been removed to reveal the structure.

Pierre Fatou. Mandelbrot had read their paper in his college days, when it represented only an obscure mathematical curiosity.

Now the computer made it possible to see the actual realization of the mathematics that described a vast array of "Julia sets." Mandelbrot's program plotted on a grid similar to the Cartesian coordinates used in high school geometry, except it included complex numbers with their imaginary component. As the first crude version of his program ran, it created a symmetrical array of disks. However, after refining the program to calculate in finer increments, Mandelbrot seemed to see what appeared to be fuzzy clumps of tiny dots. At first he thought that there was a problem with the computer's numeric routines, but when he got some time on a bigger IBM machine, the fuzzy dots, like a distant galaxy in a more powerful telescope, resolved into an intricate array of spiral tendrils!

The Mandelbrot set's prickly spirals and glowing filaments (on a graphics screen) provide endless vistas at any level of detail. Yet the whole object results from the iterative, or repeated, solving of a single, not terribly difficult, equation. It is a child of the computer age, one of the first signs that the increasingly powerful machines were making it possible to generate endless complex patterns from simple rules.

By the 1980s, Mandelbrot had become a popular lecturer. Since introducing it in a 1967 paper, he often used the ever-unfolding zooming in on the coastline of Britain as an easy-to-grasp visualization of fractal geometry. The coastline is a fractal. Instead of having only one dimension (as a line on a map), it has a fractional dimension of about 1.2. Put another way, it stuffs many extra zigs and zags into its single dimension of space.

Finding Applications

Even as colorful fractal images began to be seen in the media, many scientists were slow to realize and accept the general applicability

---

Connections: Generating and Applying Fractals

Since the 1960s, many different types of fractals have been discovered. Each has an equation that generates a series of complex numbers—numbers that contain both "normal" values and "imaginary" numbers, such as the square root of –1. Imaginary numbers were developed in order to make the system of mathematics consistent and complete, but they turned out to also correspond to many natural phenomena.

When Mandelbrot first started generating fractals, he had to use IBM mainframe computers that had to be fed with punch cards. Today any desktop PC can generate fractal images with ease and show them on the screen in full color.

There are a variety of free or low-cost software programs that allow PC users to experiment with fractals on their own. More sophisticated programs (including filters for Adobe Photoshop) can generate fractals from images or textures. Because of their deep but constantly varying structure, fractals have often been used to generate terrain for science fiction movies and video games as well as in digital art.

of Mandelbrot's ideas. After all, the existing statistical methods worked pretty well for most applications and resulted in neat and comprehensible charts and graphs. Fractals and chaos theory involved strange shapes and distributions that were determined yet unpredictable—and a new kind of mathematics. People trained in classical geometry sometimes lacked Mandelbrot's intuitive ability to make sense of strange-yet-familiar shapes.

OTHER SCIENTISTS: CHRISTOPHER SCHOLZ

Earth scientist Christopher Scholz began studying the distribution of earthquakes in the 1960s. Scholz and other seismologists had known for some time that earthquakes followed a clustering pattern that was reproduced at different scales. No one knew what the significance of the pattern was, nor what mechanism might be causing it, but by the late 1970s, Scholz had decided that he wanted to find out more.

Scholz had heard a bit about Mandelbrot and his work when he was at MIT, but in 1978, Scholz saw a book full of beautiful illustrations and unfamiliar equations. The book was Mandelbrot's *Fractals: Form, Chance, and Dimension.* While Mandelbrot served up an amazing array of ideas and speculations, Scholz was not sure at first how any of it might apply to the earthquake problem. He began, however, by noting how thoroughly fractal the Earth is. He considered all the cracks on or below the surface of the Earth—including earthquake faults—where fractal structures through which liquids and pressures flowed. Fractal geometry turned out to be ideal for describing these structures and interactions. As Scholz notes in James Gleick's *Chaos: Making a New Science,*

> It's a single model that allows us to cope with the range of changing dimensions of the earth. It gives you mathematical and geometrical tools to describe and make predictions. Once you get over the hump, and understand the paradigm, you can start measuring things and thinking about things in a new way. You see them differently. You have a new vision. It's not the same as the old vision at all—it's much broader.

By the 1970s, Mandelbrot and other researchers had applied their theories of fractal geometry and chaotic behavior to many aspects of nature. In biology, for example, fractals have been shown to be related to such things as the structure of a fern, the growth of bacterial cultures, and even the branchings of the human circulatory system. Astronomers found fractal structures in the rings of Saturn and in clusters of galaxies.

This head of Romanesco broccoli reveals a very clear fractal structure in three dimensions. Note how each smaller level repeats the same general type of structure. (Public domain photo, www.pdphoto.org)

Practical technologies have also been based on fractals. Photos can be analyzed to distinguish natural from artificial structures, because the former have fractal structures. Fractal techniques can also be used to compress digital images by replacing repeated structures with appropriate formulas.

Popularizing Fractals

Mandelbrot made a considerable contribution to the popularization of fractals with his books *Fractals: Form, Chance, and Dimension* (1977) and *The Fractal Geometry of Nature* (1982), which included examples such as snowflakes, mountains, and of course, coastlines. In the latter book, Mandelbrot explained how he had persevered in his search for new phenomena:

> *I started looking in the trash cans of science for such phenomena, because I suspected that what I was observing was not an exception but perhaps very widespread. I attended lectures and looked in*

I WAS THERE: EGO OR NECESSITY?

Mandelbrot's efforts may have been hampered by what some other mathematicians saw as his egotism and interest in self-promotion. Some believed that by claiming his discovery to be revolutionary he was overreaching. (This would also be said of Stephen Wolfram; see chapter 10, "A New Kind of Science.")

In his book *Chaos*, science writer James Gleick suggests that Mandelbrot saw himself as an outsider in the mathematical world and perhaps insecure about his position:

Unquestionably, in his years as a professional heretic, he honed an appreciation for the tactics as well as the substance of scientific achievement. Sometimes when articles appeared using ideas from fractal geometry he would call or write the authors to complain that no reference was made to him or his book.

Gleick quotes Mandelbrot's colleague David Mumford's admission that "of course [Mandelbrot] *is* a bit of a megalomaniac, he has this terrible ego, but it's beautiful stuff he does, so most people let him get away with it." But another colleague provides some justification for Mandelbrot's behavior:

He had so many difficulties with his fellow mathematicians that simply in order to survive he had to develop this strategy of boosting his own ego. If he hadn't done that, if he hadn't been so convinced that he had the right visions, then he would never have succeeded.

In his entry for *Who's Who*, Mandelbrot provided his own justification:

Science would be ruined if (like sports) it were to put competition above everything else, and if it were to clarify the rules of competition by withdrawing entirely into narrowly defined specialties. The rare scholars who are nomads by choice are essential to the intellectual welfare of the settled disciplines.

unfashionable periodicals, most of them of little or no yield, but once in awhile finding some interesting things. In a way it was a naturalist's approach, not a theoretician's approach. But my gamble paid off.

Achievements

As people working in different fields of science began to acknowledge the importance of Mandelbrot's work, he received a number of awards (including the Barnard Medal in 1985) as well as being elected to the American Academy of Arts and Sciences (1982) and the National Academy of Sciences (1987).

Mandelbrot retired from IBM in 1987, joining the mathematics faculty at Yale University. He retired from Yale in 2005 but later that year was appointed Battelle Fellow at the Pacific Northwest National Laboratory. In his later years, he received new honors, including the Wolf Prize for Physics (1993), the Japan Prize (2003), and the Einstein Lectureship of the American Mathematical Society (2006).

Through his long career, Mandelbrot has continued to seek out new ways to apply fractal analysis to phenomena, both natural and economic.

When considered as part of the larger context of chaos theory, there is much to justify Mandelbrot's claims to have achieved a revolutionary breakthrough in understanding the dynamic world around us.

Chronology

1924	Benoît Mandelbrot is born in Warsaw, Poland, on November 20
1936	The threat of Nazism leads the Mandelbrot family to move to France
1940	Germany invades France; the Mandelbrot family becomes war refugees
1944	The Allies liberate France; Mandelbrot begins university studies
1947	Mandelbrot receives his bachelor's degree in mathematics from the Polytechnique School of Paris

1947–48	Mandelbrot studies aeronautics at the California Institute of Technology in Pasadena and earns master's and professional degrees
1949	Mandelbrot returns to France and serves a year in the French air force
1952	Mandelbrot receives his doctorate from the University of Paris
1953–54	Mandelbrot visits the United States and is a fellow at the Institute for Advanced Study at Princeton University
1958	Mandelbrot becomes an IBM researcher and is given freedom to pursue wide-ranging mathematical interests
1960–62	Mandelbrot studies data in economics and discovers chaotic "clumping" patterns
1975	Mandelbrot coins the term *fractal* to describe his new kind of geometry
1979	Mandelbrot discovers the fractal that will become known as the Mandelbrot set
1980s	Mandelbrot's work becomes popular, and he wins numerous awards
1982	Mandelbrot publishes *The Fractal Geometry of Nature*
1987	Mandelbrot retires from IBM; he joins the mathematics faculty at Yale University
2005	Mandelbrot retires from Yale and becomes a fellow at the Pacific Northwest National Laboratory

Further Reading

Books

Albers, Donald J., and G. L. Alexanderson, eds. *Mathematical People: Profiles and Interviews.* Chicago: Contemporary Books, 1985.
    Includes a chapter with background and an interview with Mandelbrot.

Gleick, James. *Chaos: Making a New Science.* New York: Penguin Books, 1987.
> Has a chapter about Mandelbrot's work, placing it in the larger setting of chaos theory, the branch of mathematics that finds patterns within apparently random phenomena.

Mandelbrot, Benoît. *The Fractal Geometry of Nature.* San Francisco, Calif.: W. H. Freeman, 1982.
> The more technical and comprehensive of Mandelbrot's two books on fractals.

———. *Fractals: Form, Chance, and Dimension.* San Francisco, Calif.: W. H. Freeman, 1977.
> Mandel's introduction of fractals for the general reader, including illustrations and applications.

Article

"Benoît Mandelbrot: Mathematician." People's Archive. Available online. URL: http://www.peoplesarchive.com/browse/movies/2930. Accessed on July 18, 2006.
> Video and transcript of an interview with Mandelbrot covering his life and work.

Web Site

Fractint Homepage. URL: http://spanky.triumf.ca/www/fractint/fractint.html. Accessed on May 18, 2006.
> Contains documentation, tutorials, data libraries, and downloadable software for Fractint, an extremely versatile fractal generating program that runs on PC-compatible computers.

ON BUTTERFLY WINGS

EDWARD LORENZ AND CHAOS THEORY

In everyday language, "chaos" is something most people want to avoid. It can refer to a young person's untidy bedroom, a crowd that panics when a fire breaks out in an auditorium, or, for a scientist, a seemingly random and meaningless collection of data.

Starting in the 1970s, however, a group of mathematicians and scientists began to speak of chaos in a different way. Struggling to develop computerized weather predictions, a meteorologist named Edward Lorenz had discovered that supposedly orderly calculations were breaking down and spewing out wildly varying numbers. At the same time chaos was bursting out of order, a new kind of order was being found in chaos. This "chaos theory" would revolutionize the way scientists looked at many different phenomena and would have an impact as timely as today's concerns about global warming.

Clouds and Calculations

Edward Lorenz was born on May 23, 1917, in West Hartford, Connecticut. As a boy, he was fascinated by weather, faithfully recording each day's maximum and minimum temperatures from the thermometer hanging outside the family home. But young Lorenz's other source of fascination was books of mathematical puzzles. Sometimes he and his father worked on the puzzles together.

It was not surprising, then, that Lorenz majored in mathematics at Dartmouth College, where he received his bachelor's degree in 1938. He then went to Harvard University, earning a master's degree in mathematics in 1940.

Forecasting and Meteorology

Lorenz's path to a mathematical career was then interrupted by World War II. The Army Air Corps put Lorenz to work on preparing weather forecasts. In the new kind of war that was raging across the Atlantic and over Europe, knowing the likely weather for the next few ways was crucial. Accurate weather forecasts determined whether fleets of bombers would be able to find their targets. And in June 1944, it was the forecasting of a brief window of clear weather that made Dwight Eisenhower, supreme commander of Allied Forces in Europe, decide to go ahead with the fateful D-day landings.

Lorenz found he enjoyed working with meteorology. After leaving the army, he returned to MIT and earned his doctorate in 1948. During that time, Lorenz was influenced by two prominent MIT meteorologists, Carl-Gustaf Rossby and Vilhelm Bjerknes, who had developed one of the first systematic, dynamic weather models.

Lorenz then joined the faculty of MIT in the department of meteorology. While serving there, Lorenz also had the opportunity to teach and do research at the Lowell Observatory

Meteorologist Edward Lorenz discovered something peculiar in his early computer weather model: Very small changes in input could lead to very different results. His further studies led to the development of chaos theory. (Courtesy MIT Museum)

in Flagstaff, Arizona; the University of California at Los Angeles (UCLA), the Norwegian Meteorological Institute in Oslo, and the National Center for Atmospheric Research in Boulder, Colorado.

While serving as a visiting scientist at Harvard in 1950, Lorenz did research on atmospheric energy balance. Upon his return to MIT, his research would be expanded to create a joint effort between MIT and UCLA to develop a statistical weather forecasting model.

A New Approach to Weather

Although far-flung weather stations and forecasters had helped the Allies win the war, weather forecasting in the mid-20th century was not all that reliable. Meteorologists had worked out a fair amount of general theory about how air masses formed and interacted under various conditions. But translating the data they gathered from their instruments and applying some theory and a bit of "rule of thumb" did not guarantee that days predicted to be partly cloudy would not end up being rainy ones. For their part, mathematicians tended to shy away from weather forecasting because it seemed more an inductive art than a way to work out theories.

By the 1960s, however, computers were finally starting to become available for interesting scientific projects that could be tackled by a few researchers rather than a massive team such as that used in the Manhattan Project. Lorenz became comfortable with the new machines and decided that their calculating power could be used to turn the physics of air and water, heat and turbulence into a weather model that really worked. Given such a model, forecasters could input their current readings of wind speed, air pressure, cloud cover, and other variables. The computer model would then apply a set of equations reflecting the various natural laws involved and essentially generate tomorrow's weather (or maybe even next week's), giving an accurate forecast.

At the start of the computer age, people like Alan Turing and especially John von Neumann (see chapter 3, "Surmises and Simulations") had believed that the ability to turn massive calculations into accurate simulations would be one of the most promising things to do with the new technology. Lorenz decided to see if they were right.

Because computer-processing time was still expensive and memory-limited, Lorenz had to simplify his computer weather model drastically, incorporating only 12 equations. Nevertheless, things started out pretty well: The wind direction and speed, temperature, and other variables generated by the computer seemed to more or less match what an experienced meteorologist would expect, given the input data. Lorenz rigged a crude graphics system—dots printed on an unwinding roll of paper to show the trends and fluctuations in the weather variables.

A Berserk Computer?

Science is full of surprising moments, like the time when Alexander Fleming discovered what a mold called penicillium had accidentally done to his bacterial culture. For Lorenz, the surprise came one winter day in 1961 when he wanted to run a weather simulation over again to see the effects of some "tweaks." Not wanting to wait for the computer to recalculate everything from the initial data, however, Lorenz grabbed a printout that had been made about halfway through the past run. He reasoned that if he typed the values of the variables from the printout and started the computer, it would simply duplicate the rest of the previous run and leave him in a position to continue on from there.

Lorenz typed in the numbers, started the machine, and took a coffee break. When he returned and looked at the paper rolling out of the printer, however, he saw that the output hardly resembled the printout from the original run at all!

Had the computer gone haywire? No, the machine was all right. When Lorenz compared the original numbers from those he had input the second time, he realized that while for the original run he had input numbers with six decimal places, the printout he had used to type the numbers the second time had shown only three places (to save precious computer memory).

It should not have made that much difference. If, as meteorologists had assumed, weather was a linear system, a small change of a 10-thousandth or less in the input variable should have made only a tiny change in the output from the weather model. But upon closer examination, Lorenz found that the new and old output started out the same, but then one curve slowly began to lag behind the other—then suddenly they diverged completely, no longer resembling each other at all.

In 1972, Lorenz explained this phenomenon by giving the world one of today's most popular metaphors. Speaking before the American Association for the Advancement of Science, Lorenz titled his lecture "Does the Flap of a Butterfly's Wings in Brazil Set off a Tornado in Texas?" Technically, the phenomenon would be called "sensitive dependence on initial conditions"—but soon everyone was calling it the butterfly effect.

The Limits of Forecasting

This was potentially very bad news for the future of weather forecasting. By the 1960s and 1970s, forecasters were confidently predicting that they would achieve a new level of accuracy. They were relying on two new tools: powerful supercomputers to drive weather models far more sophisticated than Lorenz's early efforts and weather satellites to provide accurate, comprehensive real-time weather data.

The new generation of computers were also being used by other scientists and engineers, seeking to create models for everything from submarine propellers to jet airliner wings to forecasting the movement of commodity prices. At first hardly anyone knew of the significance of Lorenz's wildly gyrating computer weather model. But if it was not a fluke—if tiny changes in input could produce wildly varying output—then there was a limit to the accuracy of any computer model. It was a limit that could not be overcome simply by getting a more powerful computer, because it was something inherent in a wide variety of processes involving measuring and modeling. It was mathematical chaos. Lorenz announced his discovery in an obscure paper titled "Deterministic Nonperiodic Flow" in the *Journal of Atmospheric Sciences*. Since this was pretty much a specialty publication for meteorologists, most physicists and mathematicians never saw the paper, let alone grasped its significance.

TRENDS: WEATHER FORECASTING TODAY

How has weather forecasting fared since Edward Lorenz's weather model ran into chaos in the early 1960s? On the one hand, modern instrumentation provides much more comprehensive and precise data. Weather satellites make it possible to study storm systems from the perspective of 22,000 miles out in space. Sophisticated radar (including Doppler radar) can precisely pinpoint the speed and direction of moving air masses.

The quality of the weather models into which the data are input has also improved considerably. To some extent at least, chaos *can* be tamed by formulating enough complicated equations and having a supercomputer to crunch the numbers.

On the other hand, while short-term forecasts have become very accurate, long-term forecasts (more than a few days) and climate forecasting remain very difficult. In part, this is because scientists know less about what shapes climate than about what shapes daily weather.

When one gets to truly long-term questions such as global warming, the problem becomes even more difficult. Nevertheless, the combination of improved historical data and better understanding of mechanisms (such as the effects of greenhouse gases and interaction of ocean with atmosphere) has led most scientists to a consensus that the Earth is getting warmer and that human activities are playing a significant role.

Demonstrations of Chaos

Lorenz carried on, however. He looked beyond weather models to try to find other phenomena that might exhibit this lack of regularity or "periodicity." He found three relatively simple equations that modeled an aspect of convection, the process by which a hot liquid or gas rises. Lorenz found an even simpler version of such a system: an old-fashioned waterwheel in which water falls into a series of buckets. At first the wheel turns smoothly, with each bucket being filled, traveling downward by the pull of gravity and emptying its contents at the bottom. But if the speed of the water flow is increased past a certain point, the wheel is turning so fast that the

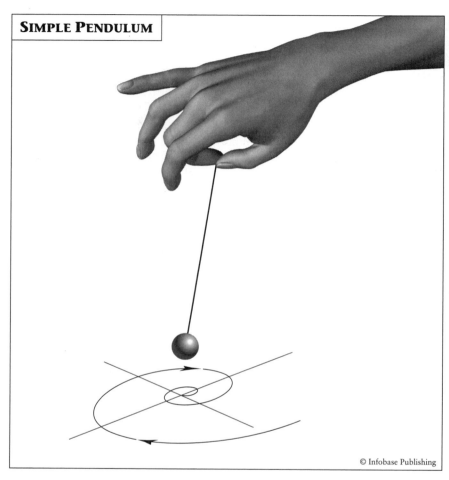

SIMPLE PENDULUM

A pendulum is a simple example of an "attractor"—however, when it is first put into motion, the pendulum's paths converge on the origin.

buckets do not have enough time to either fill or empty completely. The wheel begins turning erratically and unpredictably—possibly even reversing its direction for a time.

Another tool for chaos research was the pendulum, a very simple device more likely to be found in a children's science kit than a real laboratory. About 400 years ago, Galileo explained the overall motion of a pendulum. For example, he asserted that the period of a pendulum (the time it takes for a swing) is independent of the length of the cord by which the pendulum is suspended. Another thing about pendulums is that their motion converges gradually toward a perpendicular point. Pendulums seem to be quite well-behaved, predictable beasts.

However, Lorenz and other chaos theorists began to look at double pendulums. A double pendulum is essentially a small pendulum that moves around from the end of a larger pendulum. One might think the two motions would con╌ ╌e to form a complex but regular ╌╌╌╌ ╌ ╌s. Instead, a double pendulum

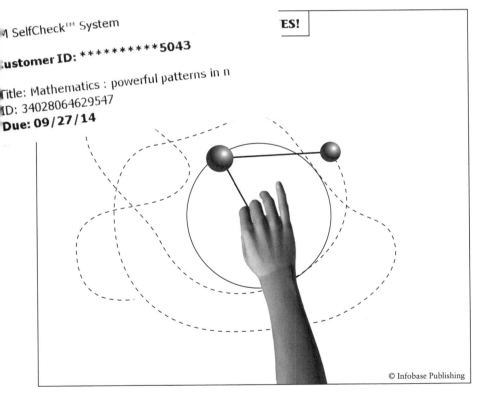

A double pendulum behaves deterministically when given a small motion, but a large initial motion produces varying, chaotic paths.

Strange Attractors

There is a popular misconception that chaos is the same thing as randomness. However, as Lorenz points out in his book *The Essence of Chaos*, there are many processes such as "the tumbling of a rock down the mountainside, or the breaking of waves on an

---

OTHER SCIENTISTS: MITCHELL FEIGENBAUM

Mitchell Jay Feigenbaum (1944–   ) is a mathematical physicist who has made important contributions to the development of chaos theory. Feigenbaum's route to the study of chaos was by way of work at the Los Alamos National Laboratory, where he studied fluid turbulence, one of the most intractable problems of physics.

In 1975, Feigenbaum discovered an equation that started out linear (that is, the output values increased smoothly in relation to the input values). However, as he continued to work with his trusty HP-65 handheld calculator, he found that as the input parameter reached a certain value the output suddenly split or "bifurcated" and began oscillating between two different values. In fact, a whole series of such splits occurred, each pair of values being farther apart. Feigenbaum discovered that the ratio between the values at which successive period-doubling bifurcations occurred was always the same number, approximately 4.6692.

Feigenbaum then proved mathematically that this bifurcation behavior (and the 4.6692 ratio) would occur in a large class of different mathematical functions. Because many of these functions could be related to chaotic behavior in a variety of natural and human phenomena, Feigenbaum's results suggested that the emerging chaos theory has a universal applicability.

Feigenbaum also worked with fractal geometry (see chapter 5, "Endless Structure") and applied it to computerized cartography, or mapmaking. The versatile Feigenbaum also generously helped his colleagues when they appeared to be stuck on a difficult problem. "Taking a walk with Feigenbaum" thus became a popular resource for Los Alamos mathematicians.

ocean shore . . . whose variations are *not random but look random.*" This is why the term *deterministic chaos* is used: At any given point, the result (the position of an object, the value of an output variable) is determined by specific forces and can be calculated. One cannot, however, simply predict the next position or value on the basis of what has gone before, because the process is nonlinear. Literally, one cannot draw a line (or a curve) and say that because the input is X more, the output will be Y farther along. However, this does not mean that there is no pattern or structure that appears as one plots point after point.

Mandelbrot found with his fractals (see chapter 5, "Endless Structure") that while each layer of detail is different, the same general structures keep recurring at each level. Similarly, Lorenz found that while chaotic dynamic systems seem to behave wildly, if one plotted the solutions to the equations on a kind of grid called phase space, the pattern of dots approached or converged upon a particular shape, which he dubbed a "strange attractor." (Regular attractors were already known, of course. For example, with a single pendulum, the attractor is the point perpendicularly below the pendulum, toward which the pendulum converges in a spiral motion.)

When Lorenz plotted his convection equations, he found that they converged upon an attractor that had a remarkable butterfly-like shape (not to be confused with the butterfly effect). Also called the Lorenz attractor, this system also emerges in models of certain waterwheels and even electric dynamos.

Chaos: A New Paradigm?

In his 1962 book *The Structure of Scientific Revolutions,* historian of science Thomas Kuhn said that the development of science combined two different processes. One was the gradual accumulation of evidence to support the current scientific view of the world. For example, physicists in the 18th and most of the 19th century saw themselves as expanding and completing the Newtonian view of an orderly, calculable universe. However, anomalies also accumulate—phenomena that stubbornly refuse to fit within the accepted theory. When enough anomalies arise, a few scientists begin to explore radically different theories. If a new theory is shown to fit the evidence better than the old one, it will eventually be accepted. Often, however, acceptance comes only after decades of resistance, and sometimes only after the innovators have risked their professional future.

By the 1980s, a growing number of scientists in meteorology, physics, biology, chemistry, and other fields were coming to believe that chaos theory was just such a new model of the world, or paradigm. Part of the justification for this claim was that chaos theory seemed to address a whole variety of phenomena that could not be

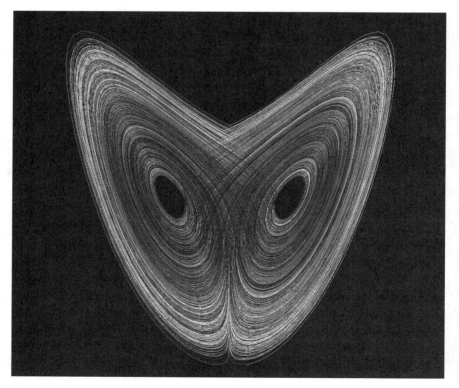

This Fractint for Windows simulation shows the Lorenz attractor. Its butterfly-like shape seems appropriate, since the flapping of that insect's wings is often used as a metaphor for the tiny initial changes that can lead to large, unexpected results.

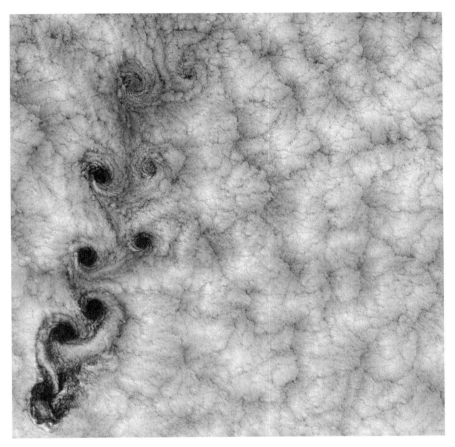

This photo shows a cloud system filled with roiling, chaotic motion. (Photo from the U.S. National Oceanic and Atmospheric Administration)

quite captured by the traditional methods of probability, statistics, and linear calculation. Indeed, science writer James Gleick quotes an administrator as remarking to his audience of scientists that "Fifteen years ago, science was heading for a crisis of increasing specialization. Dramatically, that specialization has reversed because of chaos." In other words, the universal applicability of chaos theory was enabling scientists to make new and broader connections between various scientific fields.

Gleick quotes a physicist as suggesting that chaos theory might amount to a third revolution in physics—in other words, a new paradigm: "Relativity eliminated the Newtonian illusion of absolute space and time; quantum theory eliminated the Newtonian dream of a controllable measurement process; and chaos eliminates the Laplacian fantasy of deterministic probability."

At the same time, chaos was removing a last bastion of certainty from physics, however, it was also making an exciting new kind of physics available for scientists who could not afford giant particle accelerators and the other tools of contemporary "big science." As Gleick noted: "Of the three [revolutions in physics], the revolution in chaos applies to the universe we see and touch, to objects at a human scale. Everyday experience and real pictures of the world have become legitimate targets for inquiry."

By the 1990s, chaos had become a trendy if not always accurate way to speak of how the new science was different from the old. Gleick's book *Chaos* had brought the fascinating story of chaos and fractal geometry to many nonscientists. Lorenz's own 1993 book *The Essence of Chaos* also offered a guide to his work.

Achieving Recognition

By the late 1980s, Lorenz, like Mandelbrot, had moved from an obscure, specialized corner of science into the mainstream and even the popular imagination. The affirmation of Lorenz's work by his peers gradually arrived in the form of a number of awards, including the Carl-Gustaf Rossby Research Medal of the American Meteorological Society (1969), election to the National Academy of Sciences (1975), and the Crafoord Prize of the Royal Swedish Academy of Sciences (1983).

In 1991, Lorenz was awarded the Kyoto Prize for his work in establishing "the theoretical basis of weather and climate predictability, as well as the basis for computer-aided atmospheric physics and meteorology." The Kyoto committee went on to cite Lorenz's best-known achievement: "in discovering 'deterministic chaos,' a principle which has profoundly influenced a wide range of basic sciences and brought about one of the most dramatic changes in mankind's view of nature since Sir Isaac Newton."

Even though he is now in his late eighties, Lorenz still works in his office at MIT several days a week. In 2005, he published two

ISSUES: THEORIES AND FADS

There is a tendency for any theory that is both original and far-reaching to expand to fill the available space in scientific and popular discourse. For example, Norbert Wiener's cybernetics and Claude Shannon's information theory (both developed in the 1940s) had become popular buzzwords by the 1950s, being applied not only within the engineering field where they had originated but also in psychology, social science, and even business management.

In order to become a fad, a theory must offer intriguing but graspable ideas that look like they can be applied widely. In the process of applying the ideas, however, they tend to become less concrete and more metaphorical. For example, Shannon used the term *information* in a specific technical sense that did not refer to the actual content of a message. In popular discussion, however, "information theory" became associated with general ideas such as "information is power" or later "the Information Age."

By the time a new theory is in general circulation, the question is not whether it is right or wrong but whether it is being distorted. In the book *Introducing Chaos,* mathematician Ian Stewart suggests that

> The term "chaos" has escaped its original bounds, and in doing so has to some extent become devalued. To many people, it is no more than a new and trendy term for "random." Take some system with no obvious pattern, declare it to be an example of chaos, and suddenly it is living on the intellectual frontier instead of being boring old statistics again. Chaos has become a metaphor, but far too often the wrong metaphor.

Another mathematician, Peter Allen, is quoted as suggesting that the chaotic aspect of complex systems is being overemphasized: "In reality, the important aspect is the origin and evolution of structure and organization in complex systems—not the trivial occurrence of sensitivity in strange attractors." However, Allen goes on to suggest that "chaos may be used in nature to provide 'noise' with which to maintain adaptability and surprise."

There is no doubt, however, that ideas from chaos theory (and the larger field of complex emergent systems) continue to provide important tools for research in a variety of fields.

scientific papers, "Designing Chaotic Models" and "A Look at Some Details of the Growth of Initial Uncertainties."

Chronology

1917	Edward Lorenz is born on May 23 in West Hartford, Connecticut
1938	Lorenz receives his bachelor's degree in math from Dartmouth College
1940	Lorenz receives his master's degree in math from Harvard University
1943	Lorenz earns a master's degree in meteorology at MIT
1942–46	Lorenz serves as a weather forecaster for the U.S. Army Air Corps during World War II
1948	Having returned to MIT, Lorenz receives a doctorate in meteorology
1948–55	Lorenz is on the staff of the MIT department of meteorology; he also takes leaves of absence for research or teaching at Lowell Observatory in Flagstaff, Arizona, and at various meteorological research institutes
1963	Lorenz publishes his paper on "Deterministic Nonperiodic Flow," formulating what came to be known as chaos theory
1972	Lorenz's talk at the American Association for the Advancement of Science coins the term *butterfly effect*
1993	Lorenz publishes his popular book *The Essence of Chaos*

Further Reading

Books

Gleick, James. *Chaos: Making a New Science.* New York: Penguin Books, 1987.

A very readable and engaging account of the development of chaos theory, including its development from Lorenz's work with weather and its relationship to Mandelbrot's fractals.

Lorenz, Edward. *The Essence of Chaos*. Seattle: University of Washington Press, 1993.

A popular book that expands on three of Lorenz's lectures. Lorenz explained how he discovered chaotic phenomena (particularly in weather) and developed his theories.

Sardar, Ziauddin, and Iwona Abrams. *Introducing* Chaos. New York: Totem Books, 1999.

An artistically illustrated guide to the key persons and concepts in the development of chaos theory, including numerous quotes from mathematicians and scientists.

Article

Lorenz, Edward. "Deterministic Nonperiodic Flow." *Journal of Atmospheric Science* 20 (1963): 130–141.

Key paper describing systems that are "sensitively dependent on initial conditions" and that converge on certain "attractors."

Web Site

Miguel de Campos, António. "Lorenz Atractor." URL: http://to-campos.planetaclix.pt/fractal/lorenz_eng.html. Accessed on June 22, 2006.

Interactive Java applet that generates Lorenz atractors based on the user's clicks.

7

GAMES OF EMERGENCE

JOHN H. CONWAY, "LIFE," AND OTHER PASTIMES

A visitor to the common room of the mathematics department at the University of Cambridge in the 1960s would have beheld a strange sight. He or she might well have wondered if everyone had gone crazy. Tables and floors were covered with ruled graph paper. Bunches of shells, counters, coins, and especially black-and-white Go stones were arranged in intricate patterns on hundreds of squares. A student might stare at a particular pattern and then, in a sudden burst of activity, move its pieces to form a different pattern. Other students would be arguing earnestly about things called blinkers, honey farms, and glider guns. What on Earth was going on?

The students were playing something called the Game of Life. This was no ordinary game. Its rules were much simpler than those of chess. The game had no winners or losers. Yet its inventor, John Horton Conway, would use it to show how the most complex things, perhaps even living creatures, might arise from a simple set of rules.

"I Want to Be a Mathematician"

John H. Conway was born on December 26, 1937, in Liverpool, England. Conway's father was a laboratory assistant at the Liverpool Institute for Boys, so John was exposed to science and mathematics from an early age. Young Conway quickly showed

John Conway has made many contributions to both serious and recreational mathematics. Perhaps his best-known discovery is the simple but intriguing cellular automation called the Game of Life. (Photo by Carol Baxter)

a talent for doing complex calculations in his head. His mother later claimed that he was reciting powers of 2 (2, 4, 8, 16, 32, and so on) when he was only four years old. (In later years, Conway regularly had his computer quiz him on the day of the week for 10 randomly selected dates from the past or future.) When he was interviewed for entry into high school (at age 11), he was asked what he wanted to be when he grew up. His answer was "a mathematician at Cambridge."

In an interview with *New York Times* reporter Gina Kolata, Conway reflected on why mathematics had appealed to him so strongly from his earliest years, even while challenging him to always look further: "What turned me on was this mysterious relationship between things. There is this wonderful world of logic and connections that is very difficult to see. I can see trees and cats and people, but there is this other world and it's very, very powerful."

Cambridge and "Surreal Numbers"

Conway did well in all his school classes. He received a B.A. from Cambridge University in 1959, mainly focusing on number theory. By 1964, he had earned his doctorate and had acquired a reputation for being brilliant but a bit odd. Along the way, he had also become a skilled and avid backgammon player.

Conway had also watched other mathematicians playing the subtle Asian board game called Go. Although he never really mastered the game itself, he noticed that the patterns of stones could be considered as groups for which he found analogies in number theory. Pondering this, Conway came up with a more comprehensive definition of "number" that included not only integers, rational, and real numbers but even the "transfinite" numbers that had been discovered by Georg Cantor, a 19th-century German mathematician. This new definition allowed all the tools of algebra to be applied to all these types of numbers consistently. A colleague, computer scientist Donald Knuth, even wrote a rather odd novel based on Conway's new framework, titling it *Surreal Numbers*.

Packed in 24 Dimensions

In 1968, Conway, by then married and with four daughters, was seeking to establish a firm place for himself in the world of mathematics. He would later say in the interview with Gina Kolata that "I knew that I was a good mathematician, but the world didn't." Conway was also suffering from depression, a condition that would recur throughout his career.

Conway learned that a few years earlier another mathematician had discovered an intriguingly symmetrical mathematical object that existed in a space of 24 dimensions. (Although people can actually only see three dimensions, physicists often find it useful to treat time as a fourth dimension, and mathematicians can extend their coordinate systems to include as many as they wish.)

Mathematicians who heard about this work hoped that it would lead to an advance in group theory and a better understanding of symmetry (the way in which objects have parts that mirror each other along certain dimensions.) However, there was still a great gap between the preliminary sketch of the object and the mathematical description that would make it useful. Conway was intrigued by the mathematical possibilities and wished he could take a crack at them. With a small income and four children to raise, however, Conway at first thought it would be years before he could find the time to devote to such abstruse mathematical speculation.

Nevertheless, Conway decided to devote Wednesday evening and most of Saturday of each week to developing the 24-dimensional group theory. The first Saturday, he sat down and did not quit until 12½ hours later, when he had the theory for the 24-dimensional object all worked out. The resulting structure became known as a Conway group, and it suddenly thrust him into the circle of world-class mathematicians. As he recalled to Kolata: "It catapulted me into the jet set. I remember flying to New York to give a 20-minute lecture and then flying back again."

However, unlike the case with John Nash (see chapter 4, "A Delicate Equilibrium"), Conway's great initial success did not make him anxious about maintaining his status and staying at the top of the profession. Rather, Conway told Kolata that his discovery of the Conway group ". . . had a great psychological effect. It cured my depression and it also totally removed my ambition. I've been totally successful [since], but at some level I couldn't care less. . . . I decided I that I might as well enjoy myself instead."

Puzzles and Pastimes

Conway would become one of the great creators of playful mathematics. His claim to popular fame would come not from abstruse theories that few people could understand. Rather, it would come from the way he began to present a wide variety of interesting mathematical ideas in the form of puzzles and games. (Some of the best can be found in his two-volume book *Winning Ways for Your Mathematical Plays,* coauthored with Elwyn R. Berlekamp and Richard K. Guy. It includes such intriguing [and oddly named] games as "Toads-and-Frogs" and "Hackenbush Hotpatch.") Conway insisted to interviewer Mark Alpert of *Scientific American,* however, that "I'm much more interested in the theory behind a game than the game itself."

Conway often folded bits of paper into elaborate shapes and challenged bystanders to figure them out. He created games involving geometry or topology. One game, which Conway coinvented with Michael Stewart Patterson, was called Sprouts. The rules were simple. The game starts out with a piece of paper with two spots marked on it. A player can join any two spots (or join a spot to itself) by drawing a curve, provided that the curve does not cross any curve already drawn. The player then must put a spot somewhere on the curve that was just drawn. Play ends when one player cannot draw a curve without crossing another curve or crossing a spot that is already connected to three curves.

Another one of Conway's favorite games was Philosopher's Football, or "phutball." The game used a Go board and stones. A black stone placed at the center of the board represents the ball. Players take turns either placing a white stone at any intersection on the board (to block opponent's possible moves) or jumping the ball over one or more stones in a way similar to jumping in checkers. The winner is the person who can jump the ball over the opponent's edge of the board (the goal line).

Conway's seemingly never-ending inventiveness has been coupled with a great deal of curiosity about facts, lists, and patterns—everything from the names of all the visible stars (which he learned in a year) to the first thousand digits of the endless decimal *pi*.

The Game of Life

Conway's most famous (and probably most significant) game grew out of his interest in cellular automata. During the early 1950s, John von Neumann and Stanisław Ulam had pioneered this form of simulation in which patterns of "cells" are transformed through a series of generations by applying simple rules (see chapter 3, "Surmises and Simulations"). However, von Neumann and Ulam's automata were very complex because they were designed to reproduce. There were 29 possible states for each cell.

Conway decided to see what could be done with a much simpler virtual world, in which the cells can have only two states, which can be called "on" and "off" or "living" and "dead." Each cell would evaluate its eight surrounding cells and respond according to a set of simple rules. As a result, the cell would live or die. As the pattern was stepped through many "generations," the patterns would grow, die, become fixed, or shift around on the grid of squares.

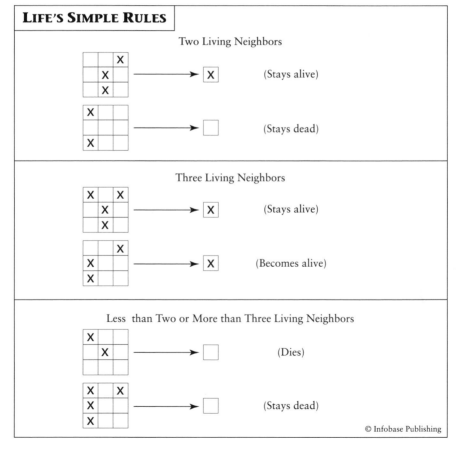

Rules for the Game of Life. The diagrams show what happens to the central cell depending on whether two, three, or some other number of neighbors are "alive."

Conway tried several different sets of rules for life and death, seeking the rules that would result in the most interesting patterns. His final rules were as follows:

- Start with a grid of cells (like a piece of graph paper).
- Mark certain cells as being "on" or "alive." For convenience, objects such as coins or Go stones can be used to mark the initial pattern of cells.
- Look at each cell on the grid. Count the number of surrounding cells that are "alive."
- If exactly two neighbors are alive, the state of the current cell does not change. (That is, if it is alive, it stays alive. If it is dead, it remains dead.)
- If there are three neighbors alive, the current cell will be alive, even if it had been dead.
- If the number of living neighbors is *neither* 2 nor 3, the cell will be dead, even if it had been alive.

Each round of checking all the cells in the pattern to see if they live or die is called a "generation." The pattern that emerges from each generation becomes the starting point for the next generation.

Conway and his students found that these simple rules produced a startling variety of patterns, depending on what kind of pattern one started the game with. A row of three living cells, which Conway called a blinker, would alternate between vertical and horizontal. An L-shaped pattern of three cells turned into a four-cell block—and after that, stayed the same forever. Some patterns, such as a T-shaped pattern of four cells, took on a bewildering variety of forms as the generations passed.

Conway called his pattern generator the Game of Life, and it was first publicized in two articles in *Scientific American* magazine in 1970 and 1971. Soon people were mailing in their own newly discovered Life patterns. As the 1970s moved on, more and more students and hobbyists were getting access to computers. The Game of Life could be easily translated into a computer program that could plot the grid cells on the computer screen or print them out on paper. By 1974, *Time* magazine was noting that "millions of dollars in valuable computer time may already have been wasted by the game's growing horde of fanatics."

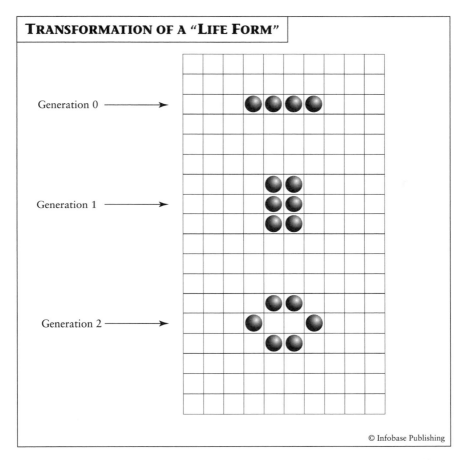

TRANSFORMATION OF A "LIFE FORM"

Generation 0 ⟶

Generation 1 ⟶

Generation 2 ⟶

A simple life-form consisting of four cells in a row generates two quite differ-ent forms each time the rules are applied to it. Each such application is called a "generation."

Life without End?

Life was not just fun and games. Serious-minded mathematicians began to ask intriguing questions about the Life universe. Was there a Life pattern that would grow bigger and bigger without ever stop-ping? Or does every pattern eventually either die out or turn into a stable configuration (where the patterns either stop moving or, like the "blinker," repeat the same sequence of forms over and over)?

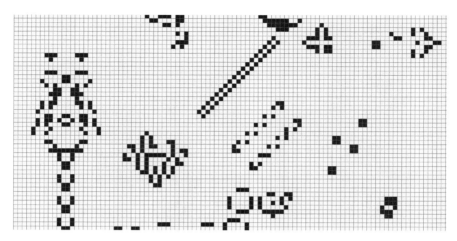

Here are a variety of different life-forms as generated by the "Winlife" program. The figure, of course, represents just a single snapshot of the ever-changing patterns.

One day one of Conway's colleagues, Richard Guy, pointed at a Life board and said in surprise "Oh, look. My bit's walking." This object, consisting of five cells, went through a series of transformations that resulted in the whole object moving one space diagonally on the grid. This object became known as a glider. The glider, in theory, might move forever.

Conway believed that if a continually growing Life pattern could be designed, it would be a major step toward simplifying von Neumann's model for a "living" machine. Conway challenged the readers of Martin Gardner's columns on mathematical games in *Scientific American* to demonstrate such a growing Life pattern.

One reader of this column, William Gosper, took up Conway's challenge. Gosper, a well-known computer expert at the Massachusetts Institute of Technology's Artificial Intelligence Laboratory, had already become hooked on the Game of Life, running thousands of generations on the lab's computers. Gosper and his MIT colleagues went to work, and in a month, they had come up with a "glider gun," a pattern that produced and ejected one glider after another. Unfortunately, the gliders eventually collided with other objects or created objects that destroyed the gun. However, by placing appropriate objects to "kill" stray fragments, Gosper was finally able to create a glider gun setup that amounted to a perpetually growing Life pattern.

Eventually, Gosper was able to show that a large, complex Game of Life pattern could actually be used as a computer, performing additions. While still nowhere as complicated as von Neumann's virtual machine, the seemingly simple Game of Life had demonstrated a new field of cellular automation and paved the way to new experiments in "artificial life" (see chapter 9, "Artificial Evolution") and to a comprehensive theory of emergent behavior (see chapter 10, "A New Kind of Science?").

This diagram shows an interesting Game of Life structure called a glider gun. The ability of the structure to generate a stream of moving gliders depends on the precise placement of certain structures that prevent "debris" from destroying the mechanism.

Seriously Weird?

A stream of interviewers have marveled at Conway's odd and unworldly quirks. In 1993, for example, well-known *New York Times* journalist Gina Kolata discovered that Conway (who had moved from Cambridge to Princeton in the mid-1980s) had recently purchased his first pair of shoes since 1969—he had worn only sandals for years, even in the rain or snow. Similarly, Conway had recently seen a barber, having decided to abandon his usual practice of keeping his hair in a ponytail and hacking off the end periodically.

Conway's work habits are also rather unconventional. As he admitted to Mark Alpert, "It's impossible for me to go into the office and say 'Today I'll write a theorem.' I usually have half a dozen things

---

OTHER MATHEMATICIANS: MARTIN GARDNER

Mathematician and writer Martin Gardner (1914–) practically created the recreational mathematics industry in the latter half of the 20th century. He is perhaps known for the "Mathematical Games" column that he wrote for *Scientific American* from 1956 to 1981. In it, he introduced the public to cellular automata (through John H. Conway's "Game of Life,"), the Hex or Nash board game independently created by Piet Hein and John Forbes Nash, puzzles involving "polynominoes," the complex "tilings" of Roger Penrose, and the world of fractals.

In addition to publishing dozens of collections of mathematical puzzles and games, Gardner has also written books and columns in his role as a champion of rationality and enemy of pseudoscience. His book *Fads and Fallacies in the Name of Science* described characteristics of pseudoscience and its practitioners (such as their tendency to use jargon and to proclaim conspiracy theories). In this and later books, Gardner took on psychics, cults, UFOs, and creationists, among others. Some critics accused Gardner of being overbroad and insufficiently rigorous in his skepticism, but his books include much material for honing and testing critical thinking skills.

OTHER MATHEMATICIANS: WILLIAM GOSPER

Better known as Bill, Gosper entered the field at a time in the early 1960s when mathematicians and computer programmers seemed to have little to say to each other. Generally, mathematicians worked at a high symbolic level and tended to view actual calculation as something akin to bookkeeping—useful, certainly, but not very interesting. Meanwhile, programmers who were learning to use a new generation of solid-state minicomputers saw mathematics as a source of tools and algorithms, but they naturally tended to be more practical than theoretical in their approach.

Enrolling at MIT in 1961, Gosper mastered mathematics while becoming one of the institution's best-known computer *hackers* (a term that at the time meant something like "computer wizard" today). Gosper made important contributions to creating programming tools that allowed for manipulating symbolic mathematics, including developing advanced tools for the Lisp computer language as well as Macsyma, a computerized algebra system.

When Conway's Game of Life was publicized, it intrigued Gosper, who then responded to the offer of a reward for designing an endlessly growing Life pattern. Gosper came up with the ingenious glider gun, which required both a moving, replicating pattern and the careful placement of small "blocks" of various kinds to cancel out drifting "debris" that would otherwise destroy the gun.

---

running through my head, including games and puzzles. And every so often, when I feel guilty, I'll work on something useful."

Richard Guy, a professor of mathematics at the University of Calgary who would coauthor several books with Conway, described the latter's Cambridge office as follows in *Mathematical People*:

> *Conway is incredibly untidy. The tables in his room at the Department of Pure Mathematics and Mathematical Statistics in Cambridge are heaped high with papers, books, unanswered letters, notes, models, charts, tables, diagrams, dead cups of coffee and an amazing assortment of bric-à-brac, which has overflowed most of the floor and all*

of the chairs, so that it is hard to take more than a pace or two into the room and impossible to sit down. If you can reach the blackboard there is a wide range of coloured chalk, but no space to write. His room in College is in a similar state. In spite of his excellent memory he often fails to find the piece of paper with the important result that he discovered some days before, and which is recorded nowhere else.

Of course Conway's quirks and habits would be of little interest if he did not continue to produce strikingly creative mathematics. Dr. Ronald L. Graham of AT&T Bell Laboratories described Conway in Kolata's article as ". . . one of the most original mathematicians . . . He's definitely world class, yet has this kind of childlike enthusiasm. He's confident enough to work on any crazy thing he wants to."

Conway continues to explore new frontiers of mathematics. In recent years, he has been trying to figure out the best way to pack a bunch of spheres into a particular space—in eight dimensions! It turns out that this seemingly abstract problem has practical uses in encoding computer data in eight-bit chunks. The eight data bits can be represented by one point in the eight-dimensional universe, given in terms of the center of the nearest sphere. Conway exclaimed that "I find it lovely that this purely geometrical thing that I'm interested in is actually useful to quite practical people." But as many other mathematicians have found, the most abstract sorts of mathematics often turn out to be mirrors of the way nature works.

In 1996, Conway coauthored *The Book of Numbers,* a sort of bestiary of unusual and strange numbers and number patterns. It is just the kind of book that might lead a young person today into a career in number theory, while enlightening and entertaining anyone who has ever wondered about hidden numeric patterns.

Although the general public knows him mainly for Life and other mathematical games, Conway has received some of the highest plaudits of the mathematical world. In 1981, he became a fellow of Great Britain's prestigious Royal Society. In 1987, the electronic engineering society IEEE gave Conway its award for outstanding paper and the London Mathematical Society awarded him its Polya Prize. In 2000, Conway received the Leroy P. Steele Prize for Mathematical Exposition from the American Mathematical Society.

Chronology

1937	John H. Conway is born in Liverpool, England
1959	Conway receives his B.A. in mathematics from the University of Cambridge; he does research in number theory
1964	Conway receives his doctorate from the University of Cambridge
1968	Conway develops the theory of Conway groups in 21 dimensions
1970	Conway introduces the Game of Life on the pages of *Scientific American;* he develops his theory of surreal numbers, helping to unify number theory
mid-1970s	Thousands of users program their computers to play the Game of Life
1981	Conway becomes a fellow of the Royal Society
1982	Conway and coauthors offer a compendium of mathematical puzzles and games in *Winning Ways for Your Mathematical Plays*
1986–	Conway moves to Princeton University, becoming the John von Neumann Professor of Mathematics
1987	Conway wins the IEEE award for outstanding paper and the Polya Prize of the London Mathematical Society
1996	Conway and Richard Guy publish *The Book of Numbers*

Further Reading

Books

Albers, Donald J., and G. L. Alexanderson, eds. *Mathematical People: Profiles and Interviews.* Chicago: Contemporary Books, 1985.
> A collection of interesting interviews that includes a chapter on John H. Conway.

Berlekamp, Elwyn R., John H. Conway, and Richard K. Guy. *Winning Ways for Your Mathematical Plays.* 2nd ed. 2 vols. Natick, Mass.: A. K. Peters, 2001–04.
> A compendium that includes many of Conway's best-known mathematical puzzles and games.

Conway, John H., and Richard K. Guy. *The Book of Numbers.* New York: Copernicus Books, 1996.
> Conway and another prolific mathematics professor offer stories and puzzles involving many famous and lesser-known types of numbers and number series.

Poundstone, William. *The Recursive Universe: Cosmic Complexity and the Limits of Scientific Knowledge.* New York: William Morrow, 1985.
> Introduces the Game of Life and relates it to larger questions about how cellular automata may relate to the structure of the universe.

Articles

Albers, Donald J. "Conway: Talking a Good Game." *Math Horizons* (Spring 1994): 6–9.
> A good introduction to Conway's approach to mathematics; includes a sidebar on the Game of Life.

Alpert, Mark. "Not Just Fun and Games." *Scientific American* 280 (April 1999): 40 ff.
> Describes how Conway's playful approach and insight into apparently simple things enables him to uncover profound mathematical truths.

Kolata, Gina. "John Conway: At Home in the Elusive World of Mathematics." *New York Times,* October 12, 1993, C1, C10.
> Interview in which Conway describes how he explores mathematics.

Web Site

"Conway's Game of Life." URL: http://www.ibiblio.org/lifepatterns. Accessed on July 12, 2006.
> The Web site includes links to background material and sample Life patterns, as well as an applet that allows users to experiment with Life within their Web browser.

8

FROM COSMOS
TO MIND

ROGER PENROSE SUGGESTS HIDDEN CONNECTIONS

By the 20th century, the power of mathematics to discern patterns in nature had expanded vastly, entering realms that would have amazed and perplexed the ancient geometers. At the scale of the very large, astronomers discovered strange cosmic structures whose elements were entire galaxies. At the extremely tiny end of things, quantum physics talked of symmetries and families of particles that spun and resonated to the tune of integers and fractions.

The world as experienced by human beings sits roughly in the center of the scale of size between subatomic particles and mega-galaxies. Nevertheless, one of the greatest mysteries in all science is found on the human scale—the mystery of consciousness. How did people come to be aware, and then to become aware of their awareness? If mathematical physicist Roger Penrose is right, there is a subtle connection between the quantum world and the patterns of neurons that make up the human brain. The human mind may be the ultimate quantum computer.

A Talented Family

Roger Penrose was born on August 8, 1931, in Colchester, England. His parents were both scientifically trained: Penrose's mother was

Physicist Roger Penrose is shown in front of a blackboard showing a cosmic "twistor." Besides his work in cosmology, Penrose has created elaborate mathematical "tiling" structures and explored the possible relationship of quantum effects to the human experience of consciousness. (Photo by Anthony Howarth/ Photo Researchers, Inc.)

a medical doctor and his father a geneticist. To the extent scientific talent might be inherited, the Penrose children seemed to be in good shape. Penrose's older brother, Oliver, would become a physicist and mathematician, while his younger brother, Jonathan, would lecture in psychology as well as becoming the British national chess champion.

In 1939, the Penrose family visited the United States. As the threat of war in Europe began to loom, Penrose's father decided to accept an appointment at a hospital in the city of London in Ontario, Canada.

Penrose's father and mother were both quite interested in mathematics, particularly geometry. Along with older brother Oliver, young Roger, not surprisingly, became interested in mathematics as well. In an interview that appeared in *Mathematics Today* he remembered "making various polyhedra [geometrical solids with many sides] when I was about ten. . . ."

Turning to Mathematics

When the war ended in 1945, the family returned to England. While his father accepted an appointment as professor of human genetics at University College London, Roger attended the associated University College School. Although his interest in mathematics continued to grow, Penrose's parents wanted him to follow them into the medical profession. Because of the way the school's curriculum was organized, Penrose had to choose between biology (needed for preparation for medicine) and his first love, mathematics. As he recalled in the *Mathematics Today* interview:

> . . . I remember an occasion when we had to decide which subjects to do in the final two years. Each of us would go up to see the headmaster, one after the other, and he said "Well, what subjects do you want to do when you specialize next year." I said "I'd like to do biology, chemistry and mathematics" and he said "No, that's impossible—you can't do biology and mathematics at the same time, we just don't have that option." Since I had no desire to lose my mathematics I said "Mathematics, physics and chemistry." My parents were rather annoyed when I got home; my medical career had disappeared in one stroke.

Since Penrose's father was a professor at University College London, Roger was able to attend that institution without paying tuition. After earning his bachelor's degree in mathematics (with first-class honors), he went to the University of Cambridge to study advanced mathematics.

Mathematical Physics

By this time, Penrose had become strongly drawn to mathematical physics. There are several reasons for this shift in interest. His older brother, Oliver, was already working in physics. Penrose had also become intrigued by various physics problems after taking a course in general relativity and one in quantum mechanics. Finally, a course in mathematical logic introduced Penrose to topics that would greatly interest him later, including the work of Alan Turing on computability and Kurt Gödel's theorem on the limits of mathematical systems. Dennis Sciama, a friend of Penrose's brother, also conveyed to him much of the excitement of the new developments in physics.

Penrose received his Ph.D. from the University of Cambridge in 1958, after having written several important papers on matrix equations. The following year, however, he would begin the work that would make him one of the world's foremost mathematical physicists. The early papers would deal with the peculiar geometry of shapes traveling at "relativistic" (near-light) speeds and for visualizing gravity in geometric terms.

Black Holes and Hawking

In 1965, Penrose applied his mathematical skills to a situation that was beginning to intrigue physics—the conditions that occur when a massive object (such as a star) collapses under its own gravity.

In Sciama's study group, Penrose met a fellow student named Stephen Hawking. Hawking had worked out some intriguing ideas about the mysterious objects that would soon be known as black holes. However, he did not know enough about the mathematics needed to translate his intuitive grasp of the phenomena into a detailed theory.

This is where Penrose was able to help. Penrose worked out the mathematics of what came to be known as a singularity—a point of zero volume and thus of infinite density. A consequence of this mathematics appeared to be that no object, or even light, could escape across the black hole's boundary, or "event horizon."

In turn, Hawking made an intuitive leap: He asked whether the universe itself might have arisen from a singularity, unfolding in that explosion that had been dubbed the big bang.

Penrose formulated what he called the principle of cosmic censorship. He said that a "naked" singularity could not exist; it had to possess an event horizon in order to isolate it from the rest of the universe.

However, in 1969, Penrose announced that black holes were not in fact completely isolated from the surrounding space. If a particle approached a black hole, it would split into two particles. One would fall into the hole, while the other would escape, transferring some rotational energy from the black hole.

Twisted Space and Tricky Tiles

Penrose's interest in cosmology extended well beyond black holes, and, starting in the 1960s, he developed several new theories. He

---

OTHER SCIENTISTS: STEPHEN HAWKING

After Albert Einstein, Stephen Hawking (1942–) is probably the world's best-known physicist. Despite being severe disabled from amyotrophic lateral sclerosis (ALS, or Lou Gehrig's disease), Hawking has been able to revolutionize the understanding of cosmology.

In collaboration with Roger Penrose, Hawking developed and expanded a theory that related a mathematical construct called a singularity to the conditions within infinitely dense black holes. Hawking and Penrose also created a new model of curved but unbounded space-time, with the initial big bang at one pole and possibly a convergence ("big crunch") at the other pole. In later research, Hawking revised some of his earlier theories about black holes. In particular, he now believes that information about an object sucked into a black hole is not actually lost; it eventually emerges in garbled form.

Hawking has been able to live a very full and active life despite his paralysis. He was aided by his first wife, Jane (and later, a series of nurses); a sophisticated motorized wheelchair, and a computer with a voice synthesizer.

Hawking has a strong belief that the educated public should also be able to understand the new cosmology and to appreciate its significance. His 1988 book *A Brief History of Time* and a later film documentary became surprisingly popular. Hawking has also recently been reported as planning to write a children's book "like Harry Potter, but without the magic."

Hawking was remarried in 1995, to Elaine Manson, one of his nurses. The couple filed for divorce in late 2006.

started with a mathematical construct called a twistor—a massless object that had both linear and angular momentum and that moved in a special form of "twistor space." Penrose tried to show how the laws of modern physics could be expressed in terms of twistors. His book *Spinors and Space-Time* (coauthored with W. Windler and published in two volumes in 1984 and 1986) gave the fullest account of the theory. Most physicists today do not believe that the twistor theory is the most useful for describing the universe, being more inclined to look toward various forms of string theory.

Meanwhile, in 1974, Penrose introduced an innovation in "tiling," or the process of trying to fill a space completely by a suitable arrangement of repeated, regular figures. Mathematicians knew that triangles, squares, and hexagons could fill an area without leaving any spaces between them (consider, for example, the arrangement of hexagonal cells in a honeycomb.) However five-sided figures (pentagons) inevitably left a crack when three were fit together. Scientists who studied crystals also knew that no crystals had fivefold symmetry.

Penrose, however, developed a new form of tiling. He began by constructing two rhombuses from a regular parallelogram, dividing the diagonal by a golden section (thus harkening back to the Greeks; see chapter 1, "How Nature Counts"). The rhombuses could then be arranged so that no configuration was exactly repeated, but the whole plane was covered. These tiles had almost perfect fivefold symmetry.

At first "Penrose tiling" was just an interesting topic for recreational mathematics columns such as the one edited by Martin Gardner in *Scientific American*. However, in 1984, Israeli crystallographer Dany Schechtman and his colleagues (working at the U.S. Bureau of Standards) discovered that a rapidly cooled aluminum-manganese alloy formed crystals that had a fivefold symmetry! These so-called quasicrystals were in effect a natural form of Penrose tiling, and they spawned a considerable amount of scientific interest.

The Physics of Consciousness

Toward the end of the 1980s, Penrose entered a different arena, the debate about the physical nature of human consciousness. Many

PENROSE TILING

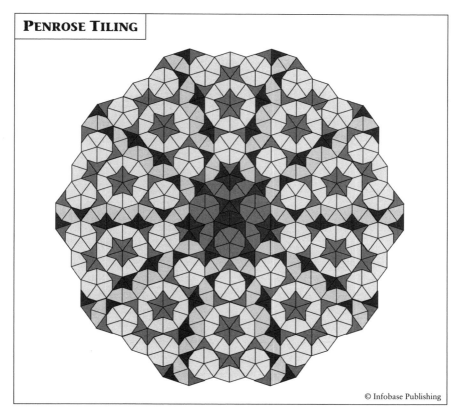

© Infobase Publishing

A "cartwheel" Penrose tiling featuring decagons (10-sided figures). Every point in every tiling is surrounded by its own decagon.

physicists and biologists tend to shy away from such questions, but they are hard to escape. In his 1989 book *The Emperor's New Mind,* Penrose notes that "Consciousness . . . is the phenomenon whereby the universe's very existence is made known." Decades earlier, quantum physicists such as Erwin Schrödinger had shown that the role of an observer could not be removed from the description of reality. But what physical processes underlie the observing mind?

By the 1980s, there was one scientific field where many practitioners thought they had the answer to that question. Artificial intelligence (AI) researchers such as John McCarthy and Marvin Minsky believed that the abilities that seemed to make the human brain unique could be replicated by a sufficiently powerful computer that was provided with the appropriate types of procedures, or algorithms. In principle, then, there was no important difference between how a human—a mathematician, for example—and some future computer might solve a problem.

In *The Emperor's New Mind*, however, Penrose argued that the view of the AI researchers was fundamentally wrong. He pointed

---

CONNECTIONS: UNIFYING RELATIVITY AND QUANTUM MECHANICS

The great backdrop for the drama of 20th- (and now 21st-) century physics has been the attempt to find a way to bring together the theory of quantum mechanics (which deals with the tiny world within the atom) and Einstein's theory of general relativity, which superseded Newton's mechanics as a comprehensive theory of time, space, and motion.

Both quantum mechanics and relativity give extremely precise results when applied to their respective realms. The attempt to fit the two theories together has foundered, however, over the problem of explaining gravity, that ubiquitous but mysterious force that binds humans and all the objects they see, but seems almost negligible at the subatomic level.

The attempt to create a grand unified theory from the quantum and relativistic frameworks partly succeeded in the later 20th century, with the development of quantum field theory that can explain the strong and weak nuclear binding forces plus the electromagnetic force.

The fourth fundamental force, gravity, has continued to resist unification. This would be a theory of quantum gravity, and Roger Penrose has attempted to work toward that theory from his twistor geometry. The current best candidate for a unifying principle may be string theory, which replaces fundamental particles with tiny loops of space-time that vibrate at specific resonant frequencies and from which larger structures and effects (such as gravity!) might be derived. Frustratingly, however, current string (or superstring) theories, while mathematically consistent and often elegant, seem to lack a practical way of verifying them experimentally.

out that Gödel had already shown that it was not possible for there to be "one universally formal system . . . equivalent to all the mathematicians' algorithms for judging mathematical truth." This meant that understanding a mathematical truth involved something beyond what was in the mathematical system itself. Penrose suggested that the mind "sees" the truth of a mathematical proposition as a whole, not simply by applying a series of algorithms to draw an ultimate conclusion.

Penrose also echoes the thought of the ancient Greek philosopher Plato. While many people today assume that mathematics represents an abstract or idealized representation of reality, Plato believed that perceived "reality" was an imperfect, distorted manifestation of the perfect truths of mathematics. Like Plato, Penrose might say that humans perceive mathematical truth because the very structure of their minds necessarily reflects it.

Is the Mind a Quantum Computer?

If the mind works differently from a computer, though, what is the basis of its operation? In later books such as *Shadows of the Mind* (1994), Penrose has attempted to suggest how the brain might be able to think in a holistic or non-algorithmic way. Conventional computers (even those with multiple processors operating simultaneously) are organized in a basically linear way. Each memory cell is linked only to one or two others. Each of the brain's trillions of neurons, however, can be connected to its neighbors in up to several hundred different ways.

Artificial intelligence researchers acknowledge the difference in complexity between the brain and current computers but argue that it can be overcome, either by simulating the brain's style of connectivity on the computer (through so-called neural networks) or by combining sufficient processing power and logical algorithms, perhaps aided by a huge database that formalizes the many facts that even a five-year-old human knows about the world.

Penrose, however, suggests that there must be a link between structures in the brain and effects taking place at the quantum level.

If so, the brain, like the quantum computers that researchers are beginning to design, has a whole additional level of power. Unlike the case of a normal computer memory location that can hold only one data value at a time, each bit of storage in a quantum computer can simultaneously store many bits.

Because even a tiny neuron is orders of magnitude larger than the subatomic particles studied by quantum physicists, many scientists do not believe that quantum effects could have any significance for the operation of the brain. Penrose, however, has focused on structures called microtubules located within the neurons. Working with medical researcher Stuart Hameroff, Penrose has tried to sketch out a model where the "quantum coherence" could be maintained even in this relatively large structure, allowing the brain to maintain multiple states at the same time.

ISSUES: PENROSE AND HIS CRITICS

Roger Penrose's provocative theories about the nature of consciousness and its possible connection to quantum physics have sparked a considerable debate. One critic, physicist Max Tegmark, calculated that the time it takes for neurons to "fire" and communicate in microtubules is at least 10,000,000,000 times slower than the time it would take any set of quantum data in the brain to "decohere" and be lost. Penrose's colleague Stuart Hamerhoff in turn has argued that there are flaws in Tegmark's analysis, and the debate continues in the pages of various physics journals.

Meanwhile, artificial intelligence (AI) researchers have attacked the other leg of Penrose's argument—the assertion that computers cannot replicate the thought processes of the brain. Although most do not believe the brain can do quantum computing, if it can, then there is no reason to suppose some future electronic computer will not have the same capabilities. Further, inventor and futurist Ray Kurzweil notes that the rate of growth in computing capability is exponential such that if the brain turns out to be thousands of times more complex than is currently believed, it would only delay by a few decades the time when the computer overtakes the brain in terms of sheer capacity.

Major Achievements

Penrose has received many prestigious science awards. In 1972, he was elected a fellow of the Royal Society of London. In 1988, he shared the Wolf Foundation Prize for Physics with Stephen Hawking. In 1990, Penrose received the Albert Einstein Medal for outstanding work relating to relativity. Later awards include the Naylor Prize of the London Mathematical Society (1991) and the De Morgan Medal in mathematical physics (2004). Also, Penrose became "Sir Roger" in 1994 when he was knighted by Queen Elizabeth II.

The London Mathematical Society accompanied its award with a citation of Penrose for his major contributions to general relativity and the understanding of black holes, as well as for

Other AI researchers believe that by focusing on logic and algorithms, Penrose is ignoring many other techniques that are showing promise. These include "bottom-up" designs where sophisticated behaviors emerge from relatively simple rules, and genetic or evolutionary programming (see chapter 9, "Artificial Evolution"). These techniques, in principle, do not require that the human designer truly understand the intelligence he or she is trying to model, but only create the conditions for the process of machine evolution to begin.

Finally, Penrose's old colleague Stephen Hawking has weighed in, contributing the chapter "The Objections of an Unashamed Reductionist" to Penrose's book *The Large, the Small, and the Human Mind.* In terms of philosophical approach, Hawking says that Penrose is a Platonist (believing physical reality is an approximation of ideal reality), while he is a positivist who believes that the ideas found in theories are only approximations of reality—hopefully ones good enough to allow for the making of predictions. Hawking goes on to say that Penrose has not given any real evidence for his novel interpretation of quantum mechanics in relation to consciousness. For his part, Penrose has not backed down in the face of criticism. The debate continues, perhaps awaiting more experimental data.

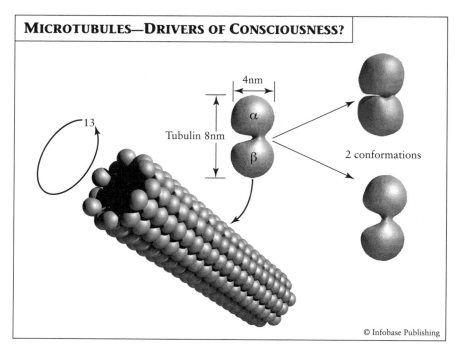

MICROTUBULES—DRIVERS OF CONSCIOUSNESS?

4nm

Tubulin 8nm

α

β

13

2 conformations

© Infobase Publishing

Penrose has suggested that structures called microtubules might serve as a sort of quantum computer "switching unit" within the brain. Penrose believes that this capability may account for consciousness, a phenomenon that has so far not been replicated in a computer or robot.

his Twistor theory and his unique and surprisingly productive approach to tiling.

Chronology

1931	Penrose is born on August 8 in Colchester, Essex, England
1939–45	The Penrose family stays in Canada for the duration of the war
1957	Penrose receives his Ph.D. in mathematics from the University of Cambridge
1965	Working with physicist Stephen Hawking, Penrose proves that a collapsing star could produce a "singularity," or black hole

1967	Penrose devises the twistor theory to map objects in four-dimensional space-time
1970s	Penrose develops censorship conjectures to suggest how the universe in effect protects itself from the effects of black holes
	Penrose describes spin networks, which later develop into a theory of space-time with loop quantum gravity
1972	Penrose is elected a fellow of the Royal Society
1973	Penrose accepts a professorship at Oxford University
1974	Penrose discovers Penrose tilings
1984	Penrose and Wolfgang Rindler began to publish a theory explaining space-time geometry using structures called spinors and twisters
1989	Penrose's book *The Emperor's New Mind* argues that existing physics cannot explain human consciousness; his views are updated in subsequent publications through the 1990s
2004	Penrose offers a comprehensive book on the laws of physics called *the Road to Reality*

Further Reading

Books

Penrose, Roger. *The Emperor's New Mind: Concerning Computers, Minds, and the Laws of Physics*. New York: Oxford University Press, 1989.
> Penrose argues that human consciousness cannot be explained by current physics or truly emulated by current computers.

———. *The Large, the Small, and the Human Mind*. New York: Cambridge University Press, 1997.
> Continues Penrose's arguments for the uniqueness of consciousness, with replies by Stephen Hawking and other critics.

———. *The Road to Reality: A Complete Guide to the Laws of the Universe*. London: Jonathan Cape, 2004.
> A comprehensive but rather formidable exposition of the framework of physics.

Article

Penrose, Roger. "Science and the Mind." Available online. URL: http://online.kitp.ucsb.edu/online/plecture/penrose. Accessed on July 20, 2006.
    Include slides and streaming or downloadable audio.

Web Site

Dutch, Steven. "Penrose Tiles." University of Wisconsin–Green Bay. URL: http://www.uwgb.edu/dutchs/symmetry/penrose.htm.
    Illustrates and describes a variety of Penrose tilings and their remarkable properties.

9

ARTIFICIAL EVOLUTION

CHRISTOPHER LANGTON CREATES VIRTUAL LIFE

Scientists face a fundamental handicap when it comes to determining the essential characteristics that distinguish living organisms from other types of systems. The Earth is home to an incredible

Computer scientist Christopher Langton popularized a field of research called artificial life. It involves the creation or simulation of "organisms" that can compete, evolve, and cooperate. (Photo © Jill Fineberg)

variety of organisms ranging from worms to birds to whales to people—not to mention strange life-forms such as slime molds and viruses that are "sort of" alive.

In defining what it means to be alive, one can say that all the organisms on the list respond to their environment, grow, reproduce, and eventually die. But how did the first living systems emerge? The problem with life is that scientists thus far have only one environment—Earth—and one evolutionary history to examine. Perhaps someday spacefarers (or automated probes) will bring back examples of life-forms that are strikingly different from those on Earth—or perhaps reassuringly similar. But until then, is science doomed to have a limited perspective on life?

Not necessarily. With the development of the computer in the mid-20th century came a tool that can not only calculate to specifications but also simulate any system that can be adequately defined. Starting in the 1980s, a group of researchers led by mathematician and computer programmer Christopher Langton began an ambitious project to create artificial life in the virtual environment of the computer.

As Langton says in a paper quoted in science writer Steven Levy's fascinating book *Artificial Life*:

> *The ultimate goal of the study of artificial life would be to create "life" in some other medium, ideally a virtual medium where the essence of life has been abstracted from the details of its implementation in any particular model. We would like to build models that are so life-like that they cease to become models of life and become examples of life themselves.*

A Dilettante Gets a Computer

Christopher Langton was born in Cambridge, Massachusetts, in 1948. Langton's father was a physicist, while his mother, Jane, had an astronomy degree and had made a modest name for herself as an author of children's books and mysteries.

Although Langton's family and their location (not far from the Massachusetts Institute of Technology) would seem to predispose him toward a scientific career, by the time he had to choose a college, the 1960s were in full stride, and rebellion was in the air. Nevertheless, Langton had enjoyed sneaking some time on the computer at his father's workplace. He also listened when his high school counselor told him that Rockford College in Illinois was about to buy an expensive computer.

Deciding that it was the place to be, Langton entered Rockford, only to find that it was a very conservative institution, while Langton was long-haired and strongly against the war that was raging in Vietnam. When Langton dropped out of Rockford, he found that he was about to be drafted. Fortunately, he obtained conscientious objector status and began to perform his alternative service at the Massachusetts General Hospital in Boston.

Langton started out as a morgue assistant, but when after a week a "corpse" he was wheeling into the autopsy room suddenly sat up, he asked for a different assignment. Langton ended up in the computer room of the Stanley Cobb Laboratory for Psychiatric Research.

Langton thrived as he learned to program a DEC PDP minicomputer to interpret brain scans and analyze other data. He reveled in the machine's ability to organize data and transform it into insights. Langton's computing experience soon reached a new level when he was assigned to create a virtual machine—a simulation that would allow the PDP to run programs that had been written for a different model of computer.

Discovering "Life"

A little later, some visiting MIT programmers brought a program that played John Conway's Game of Life (see chapter 7, "Games of Emergence"). Langton was fascinated by the blinkers and gliders and other "Life-forms" evolving on the screen. Late one night when Langton was alone in the lab, he left Life running on the machine and went about some other work. Suddenly, he felt a strange presence in the room. Looking at the screen, he saw a new and unexpected configuration of glowing cells. As he later told author Steven Levy:

> *It was the first hint that there was a distinction between hardware and the behavior it could support. . . . You had the feeling that there was really something very deep here in this little artificial life universe and its evolution through time. We had a lot of discussion about whether the [Life] program could be open-ended—could you have a universe in which life could evolve?*

In 1972, the hospital computer lab closed. Langton drifted for a while and then ended up in Puerto Rico, where he programmed a computer for the Caribbean Primate Research Center. There he found the animals at least as fascinating as the machine, and he lingered awhile to observe their behavior.

Langton had begun to realize that he needed more formal scientific training if he were to develop his still rather vague ideas about artificial life. He took a few mathematics and physics courses at Boston University and then decided to enroll at the University of Arizona. Along the way, however, he and some friends stopped to indulge in one of their favorite sports—hang gliding. Unfortunately, Langton ran into a wind shear while making a landing. He was smashed into the ground, sustaining broken arms and legs, a crushed face, and a collapsed lung.

Forced to spend months in a hospital bed, Langton began to devour texts on just about every field, including evolution, genetics, and philosophy. He was enthralled by the complexity of living organisms and other natural phenomena—and by the fact that each field knew a lot about *something* pertaining to life but that there seemed to be no overall grasp of how life emerged and operated as a *system*.

When Langton was finally able to complete his journey to Tucson and enroll in the University of Arizona, he knew what he wanted to do: create and study computer simulations of life. This would have to be an interdisciplinary project drawing from the life sciences (biology and molecular biology, evolution, genetics, and ecology) and from computer science, as well as requiring a fair amount of math, some physics, and a dash of philosophy.

Genetic Programming

One of the key aspects of Langton's project would be to figure out how to simulate evolution in a computer. Cellular automatons such as those used in Conway's Game of Life follow fixed, unchanging rules. Patterns change or die according to those rules. Life, on the other hand, carries within it a description of itself—a collection of genes. As Charles Darwin first showed, life is constantly tossing up new variations, and the environment, in turn, is constantly selecting the best-fitting organisms—those that can exploit food sources or avoid predators, for example.

The first genetic programming began in the 1960s with the work of a computer scientist named John Holland. The program started with a collection of program codes that represented alternative ways to do something, such as sort text or recognize a picture. The program would let each bit of code run for awhile and then evaluate how well it did its job. Like organisms in nature, the most "fit" codes were allowed to reproduce, while those that were less efficient would die out. Langton's first attempt at simulating evolution in a computer was designed along similar lines.

In his *Third Edge* essay, "A Dynamical Pattern," Langton explains that while this form of genetic programming could be useful for specific applications, it was not a very useful tool for studying biological evolution. Langton points out that:

As genetic algorithms have been traditionally implemented, they clearly involve artificial selection: some human being provides explicit, algorithmic criteria for which of the entities is to survive to mate and reproduce. The real world, however, makes use of natural selection, in which it is the "nature" of the interactions among all the organisms—both with one another and with the physical environment—that determines which entities will survive to mate and reproduce. It required a bit of experimentation to work out how to bring about natural selection within the artificial worlds we create in computers.

In Von Neumann's Footsteps

Seeking a more robust model of evolution, Langton hit upon the work of John von Neumann, who had designed a self-reproducing automaton in the early 1950s (see chapter 3, "Surmises and Simulations"). Von Neumann's simulation had never actually been implemented on a computer, but it looked like a prototype for a computer "creature" that might actually act like a living organism.

Langton had borrowed the $1,500 needed to buy one of the new Apple II microcomputers from a friend who owned a stained-glass shop. Langton worked by day in the shop to repay his debt and also took ditch-digging jobs to make ends meet. At night, he would get up after a short sleep and spend hours programming his version of the von Neumann simulation.

Von Neumann's design had featured 29 possible states. Another computer scientist, E. F. Codd, had simplified it to work with only eight. As Langton struggled to program the simulation on the Apple, he decided that even eight states were too many. Von Neumann had insisted that his virtual organism be a "universal computer" of the type defined by Alan Turing. It should be able to perform any definable calculation.

But as Langton was later quoted as saying by Levy, "It is highly unlikely that the earliest self-reproducing molecules, from which all living organisms are supposed to have been derived, were capable of universal construction. . . ." In other words, a simulation of evolving life should start with something like bacteria, not something like mathematicians.

The "Langton Loop"

To create a simple organism with just the necessities for reproduction, Langton created an ingenious structure that became known as a Langton loop. As with von Neumann's automaton (and the patterns in Conway's Game of Life), the organism consisted of cells that had certain values, or states, embedded in an "environment" of adjacent cells. The loop consisted of an outer layer of "insulation" (cells that had a state that would not be changed by surrounding cells) and an inner layer where the patterns responded to rules that caused them to transmit the information needed to construct the organism.

LANGTON'S SELF-REPRODUCING LOOPS

```
    2 2 2 2 2 2 2 2                        2 2 2 2 2 2 2 2
    2 1 7 0 1 4 0 1 4 2                    2 4 0 1 1 1 1 1 7 2
    2 0 2 2 2 2 2 2 0 2                    2 1 2 2 2 2 2 2 0 2
    2 7 2         2 1 2                    2 0 2         2 1 2
    2 1 2         2 1 2                    2 4 2         2 7 2
    2 0 2         2 1 2                    2 0 2         2 0 2
    2 7 2         2 1 2                    2 7 2         2 1 2                2
    2 1 2 2 2 2 2 2 1 2 2 2 2 2            2 7 2         2 7 2 2 2 2 2 2 2 2 2 1 2
    2 0 7 1 0 7 1 0 7 1 1 1 1 1 2          2 1 0 7 1 0 7 1 0 7 1 0 7 1 0 7 1 1 1 1 1 2
      2 2 2 2 2 2 2 2 2 2 2 2 2              2 2 2 2 2 2 2 2 2 2 2 2 2 2 2 2 2 2 2 2

             Time = 0                                    Time = 35
```

```
                                                          2
                                                        2 1 2
                                                        2 7 2
                                                        2 0 2
                                                        2 1 2
  2 2 2 2 2 2 2 2     2 2 2 2 2 2 2 2        2 2 2 2 2 2 2 2       2 2 2 2 2 2 2 2
  2 0 1 7 0 1 7 0 1 2 2 1 1 1 1 7 0 1 7 2    2 1 1 1 7 0 1 7 0 2   2 1 7 0 1 4 0 1 4
  2 7 2 2 2 2 2 2 7 2 2 1 2 2 2 2 2 2 0 2    2 1 2 2 2 2 2 2 1 2   2 0 2 2 2 2 2 2 0 2
  2 1 2         2 0 2 2         2 1 2        2 1         2 7 2     2 7 2         2 1 2
  2 0 2         2 1 2             2 7 2      2 0         2 0 2     2 1 2         2 1 2
  2 7 2         2 4 2             2 0 2      2 4         2 1 2     2 0 2         2 1 2
  2 1 2         2 0 2             2 1 2      2 1         2 7 2     2 7 2         2 1 2
  2 0 2         2 1 2 2 2 2 2 2 2 2 2 2 7 2  2 0 2 2 2 2 2 2 0 2   2 1 2 2 2 2 2 2 1 2 2 2 2 2
  2 7 1 1 1 1 1 0 4 1 0 4 1 0 7 1 0 7 1 0 2  2 4 1 0 7 1 0 7 1 2   2 0 7 1 0 7 1 0 7 1 1 1 1 1 2
    2 2 2 2 2 2 2 2 2 2 2 2 2 2 2 2 2 2 2      2 2 2 2 2 2 2 2       2 2 2 2 2 2 2 2 2 2 2 2 2

             Time = 105                                  Time = 151
```

This self-reproducing cellular automaton is known as the Langton loop. The little numbers represent one of eight possible states of each cell, with state 8 being blank (quiet). The "time" numbers represent the generation or number of iterations of the rules.

The states were defined according to a table that might say, for example: If the current cell is in state 3 and its immediate neighbor is state 5, then change to state 7. The result of the rules and interactions would be that the loop would create another loop with the same shape and then "pump" the information needed for construction into it. Finally, the new loop would interpret the commands it had received and use them to complete the process of reproduction.

Sitting in front of the screen, Langton started the program and watched as the initial loop activated. Levy reproduced some of Langton's notes about what happened next:

> *I'm watching it now. It looks like it will also reproduce itself and I'm hoping that [the] construction arm is long enough. . . . The daughter reproduced perfectly, the construction arm is OK! Exactly the right length! The daughter reproduces too! We're off!*

While what was happening in Langton's Apple II may not have looked like much to a biologist, it was quite analogous to how living cells reproduce. The information within the loop corresponded to the sequence of instructions in the cell's DNA. The copying of that information into a new cell (the "daughter") corresponded to the splitting and copying of chromosomes. Finally, the execution of the copied instructions was like the directed synthesis of proteins that resulted in a complete new organism.

Once Langton had self-reproducing artificial organisms, the next step was to let a bunch of them reproduce and interact. In other words, he began to simulate a natural environment, or virtual ecosystem. Rather than give the simulated computer code organisms a specific task, they were left free to interact, seeking simulated food, dealing with predators and other stresses, and if they survived, creating the "gene pool" for the next generation.

A Field without a Name

Langton had demonstrated what he thought was a powerful new computer model to study biology. However, after receiving his undergraduate degree, Langton searched in vain for someone who would give him a fellowship to enable him to study a field that no one had heard of. Finally, a program called the Logic of Computers Group at the University of Michigan offered to set up a special graduate curriculum for him.

Langton had to cope with the academic turmoil that was gradually disassembling the Logic of Computers Group. The focus of the group was changing to supposedly more practical computer applications, but Langton kept pursuing artificial life experiments, aided by John Holland, a computer scientist who had pioneered genetic (evolutionary) programming back in the 1960s.

A Virtual Ant Colony

One of Langton's projects that later became rather famous was a simulation called Vants, or "virtual ants." This little V-shaped pattern of cells simply moved in the direction of its point. The rules

---

PARALLELS: ARTIFICIAL LIFE AND COMPUTER ANIMATION

Starting in the 1980s, computer workstations became powerful enough to be used to create realistic animation (called CGI) that would revolutionize the production of movies such as the various *Star Wars* sequels. The problem was that it was very difficult to create detailed "top-down" algorithms to specify how a character should behave—and executing the algorithms could heavily tax the resources of the computer.

In 1987, computer animation programmer Craig Reynolds designed a program called Boids. It used three simple rules of interaction to create a "flock" of virtual birds that, like a real flock, could maintain its coherence while going around obstacles.

Techniques using what was in effect a type of cellular automation proved to be ideal for movie animators who needed, for example, to create realistic-looking armies of aliens or spectacular space battles. Similar techniques could be used on a more subtle level to create human characters who reacted with realistic body language in movies or training simulators.

were very simple: If the cell in front of the V was blank, the "ant" continued moving forward. If the square was blue, the ant set it to yellow, then turned right. If it encountered a yellow cell, it set it to blue, then turned left. The vant thus left a trail of colored squares behind it.

A single vant was not very interesting. When more than one was added, however, some interesting behavior emerged. Vants would start to follow each other's trails, much as real ants leave trails of chemical pheromones. Sometimes two vants would begin weaving around each other, creating a spiral trail. Langton could not help but wonder whether actual social insects like ants were really living cellular automata that followed a few simple rules to construct their elaborate colonies. At any rate, Langton believed that he had proven the power of an artificial life simulation to create "natural" behavior that was worthy of further study.

Information Is Life

Meanwhile, though, Langton still had not gotten his doctorate. The now practically minded computer science department at the University of Michigan was not inclined to let Langton write a doctoral thesis based on his artificial life experiments.

Langton had read a paper by Stephen Wolfram (see chapter 10, "A New Kind of Science?") that categorized cellular automata according to their ability to generate interesting new forms. In turn, Langton was inspired to apply Wolfram's ideas to his artificial life experiments, asking the question "What characteristics lead life—artificial or natural—to thrive?"

Langton believed that the flow of information was at least one of the keys to the success of life. He devised experiments where he could use a mathematical function to control how readily information flowed from one generation of the system to the next. Langton found that this "lambda" parameter needed to be fine-tuned. If it is too low, the system was stable but unchanging, like a crystal. Set too high, the information moved *too* freely, becoming chaotic and losing the context needed to interpret it. One could think of this as an information "gas." An intermediate value of lambda, however, provided both variety and stability, allowing the most lifelike phenomena. This was the "liquid" state. Langton would coin a famous phrase to describe this vital state: "life on the edge of chaos." Somehow, after millions of years, conditions on Earth must have reached a state like this, allowing for an explosion of living forms.

The Los Alamos Conference

As for his career plans, Langton received a break when he met Don Farmer, a researcher with similar interests, on a visit to the University of Cambridge in 1985. Farmer was working at the Los Alamos National Laboratory, and he convinced his superiors to hire Langton despite the fact the latter still did not have his doctoral degree.

Langton's first job at Los Alamos was to try to make sense of a field where scattered researchers were writing papers on cellular automata, genetic programming, and artificial life in a variety of journals—and no one really knew what anyone else was doing. As Langton later remarked to Steven Levy:

> *They just started working on stuff of their own. Either it hadn't occurred to them that the same ideas were shared by others, or they had no idea how to go about finding the other people who thought the same way. The field existed, but only implicitly.*

Finally, Langton was able to organize the first conference in the field, an "Interdisciplinary Workshop on the Synthesis and Simulation of Living Systems." Taking place in September 1987, the conference inspired its participants to begin an ambitious variety of projects, much as the 1956 Dartmouth conference had launched the field of artificial intelligence. Proceedings, papers, and journals would follow in the coming decade—artificial life had become a recognized field.

Although it would take time, the world of evolutionary biology began to pay attention to the rather grandiose-sounding claims of Langton and his colleagues. Richard Dawkins, one of the world's premier experts on evolution, even wrote an evolution simulator on his Macintosh, hoping to illustrate some of the ideas for his book *The Blind Watchmaker*. Dawkins hoped that the program would provide examples of how evolution can generate amazing complexity without the need for any external designer. He deliberately kept things simple, offering the program some simple shapes that he hoped would "evolve" to resemble plants. But Dawkins was in for quite a surprise. As he recounted in the book:

When I wrote the program I never thought that it would evolve anything more than a variety of tree-like shapes. . . . Nothing in my biologist's intuition, nothing in my 20 years' experience in programming computers, and nothing in my wildest dreams, prepared me for what actually appeared on the screen. I can't remember exactly when in the sequence it first began to dawn on me that an evolved resemblance to something like an insect was possible. With a wild surmise, I began to breed, generation after generation, from whatever child most looked like an insect. My incredulity grew in parallel with the evolving resemblance. . . . I still cannot conceal to you my feeling of exultation as I first watched these exquisite creatures emerging before my eyes. I distinctly heard the triumphal opening chords of Also sprach

Artificial life in a digital environment. The self-replicating computer programs are represented by small geometric objects in various colors or shades. The "roads" represent computer memory for which the programs compete, while the lightning indicates a source of mutations. The skull is the Grim Reaper that eliminates programs that have become too "old" or defective. (Anti-Gravity Workshop)

CONNECTIONS: ARTIFICIAL INTELLIGENCE AND ARTIFICIAL LIFE

In his *Third Edge* essay, Christopher Langton talks about the relationship between two of the most fascinating projects in computer science, artificial intelligence (AI) and artificial life (AL). He points out that the two pursuits have similarities and differences:

> I don't see artificial intelligence and artificial life as two distinct enterprises in principle; however, they're quite different in practice. Both endeavors involve attempts to synthesize—in computers—natural processes that depend vitally on information processing. I find it hard to draw a dividing line between life and intelligence. Both AI and AL study systems that determine their own behavior in the context of the information processes inside them.

Langton goes on to point out that AI tended to aim at the most complex goal, replicating human intelligence. After some initial success, AI ran into difficulties with some seemingly simpler things, such as how to recognize a face, walk, or catch a ball. Artificial life, on the other hand, starts with relatively simple systems and rules and tries to see how more complex behaviors might arise from them.

In practice, AI researchers, too, have often taken this bottom-up approach. For example, robot designers Rodney Brooks and Cynthia Breazeal at MIT designed robots in the 1980s and 1990s whose behavior emerged from "layers" of relatively simple systems that interacted with the environment and each other.

Zarathustra *(the "2001 theme") in my mind. I couldn't eat, and that night "my" insects swarmed behind my eyelids as I tried to sleep.*

Artificial Life and Consciousness

Mathematics can be used to find patterns in the living as well as the nonliving world. As can be seen in Christopher Langton's work, mathematical algorithms can also be used to simulate living systems and allow new forms of behavior to emerge. Consciousness may have a connection to quantum mechanics (see chapter 8, "From Cosmos to Mind"), or it may simply emerge from the complex interactions of relatively simple systems.

In his *Third Edge* essay, Langton asks:

> *What trick is it that nature capitalized on in order to create consciousness? We don't yet understand it, and the reason is that we don't understand what very distributed, massively parallel networks of simple interacting agents are capable of doing. We don't have a good feel for what the spectrum of possible behaviors is. We need to chart them, and once we do we may very well discover that there are some phenomena we didn't know about before—phenomena that turn out to be critical to understanding intelligence.*

Like artificial intelligence, artificial life has had its times of popularity and optimism and its times of difficulty and obscurity. When Steven Levy wrote his book *Artificial Life* in 1992, the field was only about a decade old and seemed poised (like fractals, chaos, and other mathematical and scientific movements) to transform technology and the understanding of nature.

On the one hand, the term *artificial life* is not seen in the media nearly as much in the first decade of the 21st century as it was two decades earlier. But this does not mean that the work of Christopher Langton and other researchers was in vain. Techniques from artificial life research are found today in everything from sophisticated characters for online role-playing games to software "agents" that can help people find information or shop, to simulations that researchers at the Centers for Disease Control and Prevention hope might help the world deal with the next big flu epidemic. On a negative note, some of the most effective examples of artificial life are found today in the form of computer viruses and worms.

Meanwhile, the search to understand life where mathematics meets biology goes on.

Chronology

1948	Christopher Langton is born in Cambridge, Massachusetts; around this time, John von Neumann and Stanisław Ulam begin to design self-reproducing automata
early 1970s	After dropping out of college and getting a job in a computer lab, Langton is exposed to John Conway's Game of Life
1979	Langton begins to design virtual "life-forms," creating a self-reproducing Langton loop
1982	Langton begins graduate study at the University of Michigan
1987	Langton organizes the first International Conference on the Synthesis and Simulation of Living Systems at the Los Alamos National Laboratory
1990s	Artificial life activities grow through conferences and journals; Rodney Brooks and his colleagues apply similar techniques to the design of robots at MIT; development of "software agents" by Pattie Maes and others draws on artificial life techniques
1992	Langton finally completes his doctorate at the University of Michigan
2000s	Simulation of life at a detailed molecular level is under way

Further Reading

Books

Dawkins, Richard. *The Blind Watchmaker*. New York: W. W. Norton, 1996.
> A tour de force explanation of how evolution works and how complexity emerges without the necessity of an external designer.

Langton, Christopher G., ed. *Artificial Life: An Overview*. Cambridge, Mass.: MIT Press, 1995.
> A collection of papers on a variety of topics relating to artificial life.

Levy, Steven. *Artificial Life: The Quest for a New Creation.* New York: Pantheon Books, 1992.

A vivid account of the development of evolutionary software and artificial life during the 1980s, including the work of Christopher Langton and Stephen Wolfram.

Web Site

"Welcome to Zooland: 'The Artificial Life Resource.'" URL: http://zooland.alife.org. Accessed on July 18, 2006.

This site provides a huge variety of links to background materials and simulations for exploring artificial life. They range from the classic "Core Wars" to Langton's "Vants" to Thomas Ray's rich and sophisticated simulated ecology "Tierra."

10

A NEW KIND OF SCIENCE?

STEPHEN WOLFRAM AND THE UNIVERSAL AUTOMATON

Ever since the time of Galileo (and particularly, since Newton), mathematics has been used as a tool to describe the dynamics of nature—everything from the simple effects of gravity on moving objects to extremely complex phenomena of turbulent flow and the generation of weather.

The discovery of chaotic systems (see chapter 6, "On Butterfly Wings") showed that there were many phenomena that could not be precisely predicted by equations. Chaos, however, did not overturn the basic paradigm where equations were fitted to observed phenomena in order to describe and perhaps manipulate them. Mathematicians acquired new tools and understandings, but they still approached nature in basically the same way.

Stephen Wolfram created the Mathematica program, bringing the power of symbolic mathematics to the desktop. His extensive study of cellular automation has led him to propose a controversial new scientific paradigm. (Photo David Reiss/Wolfram Research, Inc.)

A mathematical physicist turned software developer, Stephen Wolfram has issued a bold challenge to scientists. Through his extensive study of cellular automata (see chapter 7, "Games of Emergence"), Wolfram came to believe that the way to approach the phenomena of nature was not to fit calculations to observed data but to find simple sets of rules that generate the complexity one sees in nature, particularly in biology. Ultimately, Wolfram believes that nature is in effect a computer that uses many simple but powerful programs, and that his approach to studying them amounts to a new scientific revolution.

Teenage Physicist

Stephen Wolfram was born on August 29, 1959, in London, England. Wolfram's father was a modestly successful novelist, while his mother was a philosophy professor at the University of Oxford. Like many children of the Space Age of the 1960s, he was intrigued by space exploration, astronomy, and physics. Unlike most preteens, however, Wolfram began to read physics textbooks, bicycling back and forth to the local university library.

When he was 13, Wolfram won a scholarship to Eton College. This famous institution is known for sports and the preparation of the sons of the wealthy for their future place in society. Young Wolfram had neither the social background nor the interest to fit into the world of Eton. Instead, he pursued his interest in science and ignored most of his other schoolwork, although he made some spending money by doing math and physics homework for his wealthier and less academically inclined classmates.

At the age of only 15, Wolfram, apparently quite confident in his ability, wrote a paper on high-energy particle physics and sent it to professors at Oxford and Cambridge. They not only responded just as they would to professional colleagues, they reviewed that paper, and it was published in a physics journal.

When he turned 16, Wolfram went to Oxford to see what the world of physics was like. As he recalled later to author Steven Levy:

I went to the first-year lectures and found them awful. The second day I went to the second-year lectures and found them correspondingly awful. On the third day I went to one third-year lecture and decided that it was all too horrible. I wasn't going to go to any more lectures.

Oxford had a very casual attitude toward lectures and classes: As long as a student passed the examination given at the end of the first year, it did not really matter what else he or she did. Wolfram did not think much of the famed Oxford dons and told them so. When the examination came, Wolfram passed it at the top of his class. Working at a level far beyond that of most graduate students, Wolfram had produced more than 25 scientific papers in little more than two years, and he earned his doctorate in theoretical physics at age 20.

Computers at Caltech

Wolfram was then invited to study at the California Institute of Technology by famed physicist Murray Gell-Mann. In 1981, Wolfram received a coveted MacArthur Foundation "genius" grant. The purpose of these awards is to give unusually creative individuals in science and the arts enough money to give them the means and time to pursue the project of their choice.

With $120,000 in hand, Wolfram decided that what he wanted to do was use computers to generate and explore the many intriguing patterns that were starting to emerge from simple algorithms. He now believed that the sheer complexity of the structures he had been studying in physics and cosmology could not be adequately addressed by creating ever more complicated equations. Perhaps his computer could lead him to a different path.

Many of Wolfram's colleagues expressed dismay at the thought of a very promising young physicist studying some sort of simplistic computer program that would appear to have little to do with the pressing problems of physics. But Wolfram believed that a new approach to using the computer to understand natural systems was well worth his essentially abandoning his physics career.

Wolfram found that existing tools for doing symbolic mathematics on the computer were inadequate, so he wrote his own program, called SMP. However when Wolfram sought to market the program, Caltech said that it owned the rights because he had created the program while working as a researcher there. Wolfram took Caltech to court but lost the case. He left Caltech in 1982.

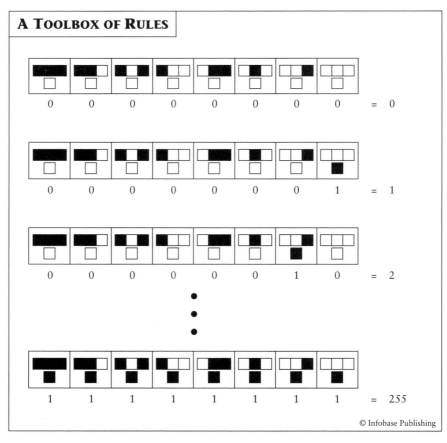

A TOOLBOX OF RULES

© Infobase Publishing

Wolfram used a set of 256 possible rules to generate a variety of types of cellular automation patterns. Each rule is numbered by converting the resulting colors to a binary number.

Studying Cellular Automata

Wolfram moved to the Institute for Advanced Study at Princeton. Unlike Caltech, they offered him a free hand in his research, plus the right to market anything he created.

By then Wolfram had become fascinated by cellular automata, the systems of rules that could generate astoundingly complex and varied patterns. John von Neumann had first formulated the concept in the late 1940s and early 1950s. Around 1970, John Conway had created one of the simplest but richest cellular automatons, the Game of Life. Wolfram, however, told author Steven Levy that "when I started, there were maybe 200 papers written on cellular automata. It's amazing how little was concluded from those 200 papers. They're really bad." (Critics would later accuse Wolfram of unfairly maligning the work of other mathematicians.)

At any rate, Wolfram decided to begin a comprehensive and systematic study of not a single cellular automation system, but hundreds. Focusing on one-dimensional cellular automata that generated one line of squares (cells) at a time, Wolfram realized that there were 256 possible rules that could be defined according to how each cell interacted with its two neighbors (behind and in front of it.)

One example, which Wolfram called Rule 110, starts with a single black square in the top row of the grid. After the computer has generated thousands of rows of black-and-white squares, however, the result is an intricate pattern that is full of both regularity and surprise.

Mathematica

In 1987, Wolfram left academia and founded the company Wolfram Research, Inc. to develop mathematics software. At the time, the computer was widely used for calculation (spreadsheets alone had sold many a PC to businesses). There were also thousands of custom programs designed to help scientists and engineers with their work.

However, contrary to popular belief, mathematicians spend little of their time actually calculating. What they really do is manipulate symbols, using the procedures of algebra, calculus, and more eso-teric branches of mathematics. Their blackboards are filled with *x*, *y*, *n*, and other letters. They simplify or transform expressions and equations. A computer program that did for symbolic math what had already been done for calculation and word processing would be a powerful tool indeed.

In 1988, Wolfram and his development team of computer scien-tists and mathematicians released the first version of Mathematica. The program has been steadily expanded and improved ever since. The system includes a "kernel" that actually applies rules for trans-formation and computation, and a choice of "front ends" that com-municate with the user and provide printing and graphing functions. Wolfram later developed versions of the software that could run on a Web server and be accessed by Web browsers, including those in handheld devices.

A Shortcut to Complexity?

Meanwhile, the more cellular automation rules he tried and the more patterns he saw, the more Wolfram became convinced that he was observing a phenomenon that was applicable . . . everywhere. As he would say later in *A New Kind of Science,* "It will turn out that every detail of our universe does indeed follow rules that can be represented by a very simple program—and that everything we see will ultimately emerge just from running this program."

One of the key features Wolfram observed is that the complex patterns arising from cellular automation are computationally irre-ducible. This means that there is no way to create an equation, plug in a few values, and see what the automation will look like after 2,000 generations. The only way to find that out is to actually run the automaton and apply the rules 2,000 times. Wolfram has sug-gested that many phenomena in nature are similarly computation-ally irreducible. If so, the proper approach to them would not be to try to come up with an equation but to find the relevant rules.

Some scientists disagree with Wolfram's conclusion, however. Nigel Goldenfeld, is a physicist at the University of Illinois at Urbana-Champaign who has studied the formation of snowflakes

and the deposition of limestone in hot springs. He and his colleagues developed an approach to complex systems that identi-
fies the broader patterns and ignores the more incidental details.
Goldenfeld and a colleague, Navot Israeli, then applied this coarse-
grained approach to the 256 types of one-dimensional cellular
automata that Wolfram had studied. They found that by grouping
the cells of the system together into supercells of eight or 10, they
could then derive an overall pattern. In turn, they found they could

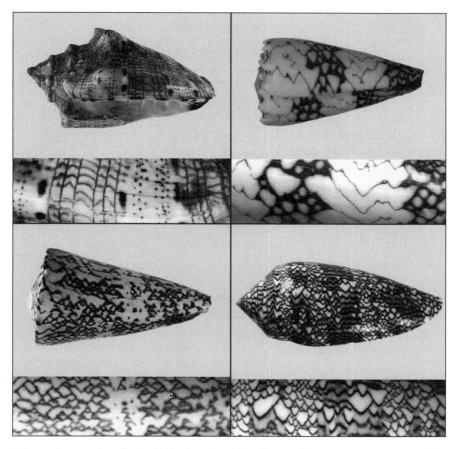

*These photos of mollusk shells show how biochemical interactions in nature fol-
low rules and yield results very similar to the cellular automatons that Wolfram
and other researchers have developed.* (Photo courtesy of Wolfram Research, Inc.)

CONNECTIONS: APPLYING WOLFRAM'S IDEAS

In *A New Kind of Science,* Wolfram suggests a number of areas where his theories about universal cellular automation might be applied. These include:

- Mathematics: adding powerful new methods to the existing approach to writing equations; overcoming the limitations of formal mathematical systems
- Physics: a new approach to building up fundamental theories from relatively simple interactions
- Biology: modeling the growth and interaction of organisms (Wolfram has also suggested that Darwinian natural selection is inadequate to explain evolution. However, creationists cannot take heart, since Wolfram's system has no place for an outside "designer," intelligent or not)
- Computer science: new forms of computer architecture and software design
- Artificial intelligence and artificial life: breaking old "computational bottlenecks" through systems where behavior emerges from relatively simple components and interactions
- Art: the generation of rich new kinds of patterns that artists can in turn interact with

---

predict the changes in these patterns even if they could not precisely specify the future state of the automaton. This approach has been used by other researchers to simplify complex, chaotic systems such as financial markets.

Universal Automaton

In trying out many kinds of rules for cellular automata, Wolfram found that there were distinct types of rules. (Christopher Langton had also discovered this; see chapter 9, "Artificial Evolution.") Some rules resulted in fixed, unchanging (and ultimately boring) patterns.

Others produced periodic or cyclic behavior (interesting at first, but then boring). "Chaotic" cellular automata changed endlessly, but not very meaningfully. Finally, the mother lode was found in the form of complex rules that have enough structure to be meaningful and enough variety to remain interesting.

The ultimate cellular automaton, however, is a universal one that can simulate any form of calculation, including another cellular automaton. This idea goes back to von Neumann, and John Conway's Game of Life provides a simpler example. However, Wolfram designed a universal cellular automaton that was particularly easy to understand and use with any sort of rules.

A New Kind of Science?

After more than a decade of intensive and mainly solitary work, Wolfram finally published *A New Kind of Science* in 2002. At its

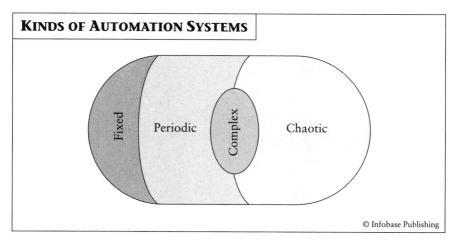

Researchers have classified cellular automation systems into four categories. Fixed systems are unchanging, thus "dead" and uninteresting. Periodic systems cycle between various forms, showing energy but little novelty. Chaotic systems are unpredictable and can produce occasional beautiful patterns, but there is little to learn from them. Finally, the category of "complex" systems produce the combination of novelty and structure that seems most "lifelike."

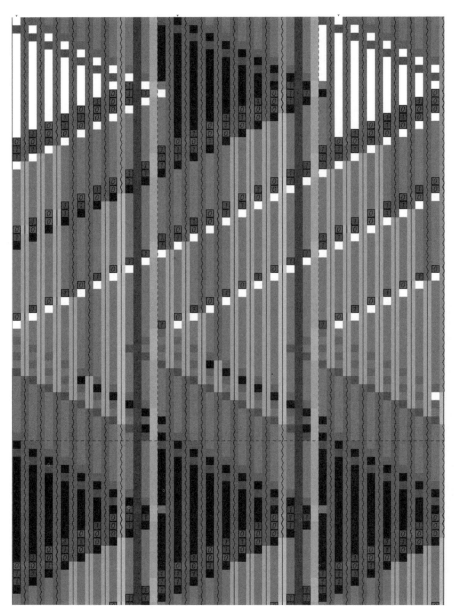

A representation of Wolfram's Universal Cellular Automaton. This automaton can, given suitable starting conditions, emulate any definable system of rules. (Wolfram Research, Inc.)

most superficial level, the hefty volume serves as a kind of coffee table book of the varieties of complex structure that can be generated from cellular automation rules.

In the preface to the book, Wolfram makes some bold statements and predictions. He begins with a claim that his work amounts to a new scientific revolution:

> *Three centuries ago science was transformed by the dramatic new idea that rules based on mathematical equations could be used to describe the natural world. My purpose in this book is to initiate another such transformation, and to introduce a new kind of science that is based on the much more general types of rules that can be embodied in simple computer programs.*

Wolfram goes on to insist that this new kind of science "touches almost every existing area of science, and quite a bit besides." Although he anticipates that there will be resistance to his ideas, Wolfram believes that they will eventually play a central role in science, technology, and other fields.

If one opens the book and looks at the details, one certainly finds a variety of provocative suggestions about how the phenomena of physics, biology, and other sciences can be reinterpreted as the behavior of automata that follow as-yet-unknown rules. These discussions can lead interested readers (whether scientists or laypeople) to think for themselves about whether Wolfram's ideas may be useful for a particular problem or application.

Reactions to the book have been mixed. On the one hand, in an interview with *Scientist* magazine, Wolfram said that many biologists have sent him e-mails that took this general form: "Here's a process in biology. It seems that your methods would allow us to understand it. What kind of comments do you have?"

Wolfram then elaborated on how he thought his work might aid biologists:

> *I think there's a tremendous awareness in that community that the next big steps have to involve theoretical modeling, and trying to*

understand global mechanisms. Questions about evolution theory often loom large in public discussions of biology. But a much greater interest among practicing biologists is to take what I've done and use it as a framework for new basic models and theories. People recognize that the genome contains some kind of program; the question is, what does that program actually do? And that is the kind of question my book gives one general methods to address.

On the other hand, participants in symposium on the book at Caltech agreed that Wolfram's book did not represent a true "paradigm shift" or fundamental change in the understanding of the universe, let alone a change in the ground rules of science itself. Wolfram suggested that the reactions of these scientists were in fact typical of the response to a paradigm shift that threatened entrenched ideas. However, moderator physicist Steven Koonin quipped in return that the reaction was also typical when the idea was *not* a paradigm shift.

ISSUES: IS WOLFRAM'S WORK PSEUDOSCIENCE?

There are many ideas (particularly in the so-called New Age community) that use the language of science but do not seem to be testable hypotheses. Skeptics call such theories pseudoscience. In his article in *Skeptic,* David Naiditch applies some criteria to determine whether Wolfram's "new kind of science" is really pseudoscience.

Naiditch says that pseudoscientists usually make grandiose claims. By his very claim to be founding a new kind of science Wolfram may be said to be making a grandiose claim. Of course Newton, Darwin, and Einstein all made grandiose claims that were later validated and accepted by science.

Another characteristic of pseudoscience according to Naiditch is that practitioners work in relative isolation. Wolfram himself admitted to being an almost complete recluse throughout the 1990s.

Naiditch also says that pseudoscientists avoid having their work reviewed by other scientists and often publish their own books.

Assessing Wolfram's Science

It is fair to say that assessing Wolfram's work as science will be difficult. Science normally uses a sort of feedback cycle where a theory suggests experiments that in turn suggest modification to the theory. Doing "Wolfram science," however, would presumably involve closely observing a particular natural phenomenon and then trying out various rules to see whether a cellular automaton can generate the same behavior.

So far, however, little progress has been made using this method. Even if that is done, does the fact that an automaton produces something like a snowflake, for example, mean that actual snowflakes are produced by the same rules?

As Wolfram would himself admit, his "new science," however revolutionary, cannot simply replace the old science that is based on formulating and using equations. As noted earlier, there is no shortcut to finding the future state of a cellular automaton. On the

Wolfram, however, has said that he wanted to wait until his work was complete and coherent rather than publishing it piecemeal where it was likely to be misunderstood. Wolfram has given similar reasons for publishing his own book even though his reputation would probably have brought interest from scientific publishers.

Wolfram can therefore make good arguments that these criteria of pseudoscience do not apply to him. However, other criteria given by Naiditch suggest that a pseudoscientist tends to not give proper credit to other scientists, instead claiming to be the originator of every relevant discovery. Wolfram's *A New Kind of Science* contributes to this impression by not having footnotes or a bibliography that would enable readers to see where his work fits into that of others.

Although certain characteristics might make one suspicious that a new idea is pseudoscience, ultimately the only real test is whether the idea actually enables scientists to obtain useful new information about how the world works. On this, for Wolfram, the jury is probably still out.

other hand, if one wants to know where the Moon will be tomorrow, simple formulas based on Newton's laws (with perhaps a slight tweak from Einstein) will give a good enough answer.

Equations also provide ways to understand more general concepts such as force, friction, or oscillation. They thus help scientists think about new problems in terms of phenomena they already understand. Wolfram's approach, on the other hand, seems to work more on a case-by-case basis. While it is probably possible to develop general concepts by finding different cellular automata to relate to different phenomena, there simply has not been enough experience to determine how best to use Wolfram's ideas.

Thus to the extent Wolfram's work flourishes, it will probably flourish alongside conventional science, offering if not "a new science," a new tool for scientists.

Meanwhile, Wolfram seems not to be bothered by critics of his work or of his personality. When asked by an interviewer from *Scientist*, "Are you modest?" he replied:

Different people have different opinions on that. It's hard to see from the inside. Certainly I am a person who values truth over modesty. For example, in my book I chose to talk quite explicitly about the importance of some of my ideas and discoveries, because without that, it would be much more difficult for people to get a correct handle on where these fit in. My situation in life has let me really be an independent scientist. And that means I can optimize communicating ideas, rather than having my colleagues applaud my humility.

Chronology

1959	Stephen Wolfram is born on August 29 in London, England
1967–72	Wolfram becomes interested in science and reads physics textbooks
1972	Wolfram earns a scholarship to Eton College at age 13
1973	Wolfram begins to write computer simulations

1975	Wolfram writes his first scientific paper (on high-energy physics)
1976	Wolfram graduates from Eton College with honors and goes to Oxford University
1977–79	Wolfram does research in quantum physics and cosmology
1979	Wolfram receives his Ph.D. in theoretical physics from the California Institute of Technology; he continues physics research
1980	Wolfram receives a MacArthur "genius" grant
1981	Wolfram begins research on cellular automata; the first version of Wolfram's SMP math manipulation software is released
1982	Wolfram leaves Caltech after a dispute over the rights to SMP and goes to the Institute for Advanced Study at Princeton
1983	Wolfram establishes a classification system for cellular automata
1985	Wolfram applies cellular automata to applications such as cryptography and fluid dynamics
1986	Wolfram moves to the University of Illinois to teach physics, math, and computer science; the development of Mathematica software begins; Wolfram publishes the journal *Complex Systems*
1987	Wolfram founds Wolfram Research, Inc.; he begins move from academia to the private sector
1988	The first version of Mathematica is released; Wolfram also writes a book to explain the software
1991	Wolfram begins work on *A New Kind of Science*
1994	Wolfram's collected papers on *Cellular Automata and Complexity* are released
2000	Wolfram's Calculation Center and Mathematical Explorer software is released
2001	An Internet-based version of Mathematica is released

2002	Wolfram self-publishes *A New Kind of Science*
2003	Wolfram organizes conferences and classes on *A New Kind of Science*

Further Reading

Books

Wolfram, Stephen. *Cellular Automata and Complexity: Collected Papers*. Reading, Mass.: Addison-Wesley, 1994.
> Collects Wolfram's papers on a variety of aspects of cellular automata.

———. *A New Kind of Science*. Champaign, Ill.: Wolfram Media, 2002.
> Wolfram's massive and profusely illustrated exposition of his new approach to science through the study of cellular automation.

Articles

Buchanan, Mark. "Too Much Information: See the World in a Blur and the Future Comes into Focus." *New Scientist* 185 (February 2006): 32 ff.
> Describes work that suggests that a coarse-grained approach can predict the future patterns in cellular automata, challenging Stephen Wolfram's argument that such automata are computationally irreversible.

Hayes, Brian. "The World According to Wolfram." *American Scientist*. Available online. URL: http://www.americanscientist.org/template/AssetDetail/assetid/13168/page/1;jsessionid=aaa6Wt PSM0X7hi. Accessed on July 10, 2006.
> A detailed critical review of Wolfram's *A New Kind of Science*.

Naiditch, David. "Divine Secrets of the Ya-Ya Universe: Stephen Wolfram: A New Kind of Science—or a Not-So-New Kind of Computer Program?" *Skeptic* 10 (Summer 2003): 30 ff.
> An in-depth critical look at Wolfram's work that argues that he is making too many broad claims about the value of modestly interesting software and phenomena.

"The Science of Stephen Wolfram: Forum." *Skeptic* 10 (Fall 2003): 25 ff.
> A forum discussing and critiquing Wolfram's work and his book *A New Kind of Science?*

Wolfram, Stephen. "Stephen Wolfram." *The Scientist,* 17, no. 7 (April 2003): 11.
  Brief interview in which Wolfram describes what motivates his work and responds to the reaction of other scientists to it.

Web Sites

A New Kind of Science. URL: http://www.wolframscience.com. Accessed on July 5, 2006.
  The official Web site for Stephen Wolfram's book of the same name, including supplemental material and news.
Stephen Wolfram. URL: http://www.stephenwolfram.com. Accessed on July 5, 2006.
  Official Web site for Stephen Wolfram, including biographical and background material, papers, and lectures.

CHRONOLOGY

sixth century B.C.	Pythagoras and his school teach that true reality is revealed by mathematics
fourth century B.C.	The Greek Parthenon is built using the golden ratio
eighth and ninth centuries	Arab mathematicians adopt Indian numerals (1–9 and 0) and develop algebra
1202	Leonardo of Pisa introduces Arabic numerals to Europe with his book *Liber Abaci*
14th and 15th centuries	The Renaissance leads to application of mathematics to art and architecture
17th century	Galileo Galilei and Kepler apply mathematics to physics and astronomy; Newton and Leibniz invent calculus
1892	Karl Pearson publishes *The Grammar of Science*
1900	Pearson founds the journal *Biometrika* to promote modern statistical techniques in biology and other sciences
1939–45	World War II stimulates the development of the computer
1944	John von Neumann and Oskar Morgenstern publish their book on *The Theory of Games and Economic Behavior*
1945	Von Neumann's draft report on EDVAC outlines the features of the modern electronic digital computer

1948	Von Neumann and Stanisław Ulam begin to work on cellular automata
1950	John Nash publishes a key game-theory paper, "The Bargaining Problem"
1953	Nash publishes a paper, "Two Person Cooperative Games"
1963	Edward Lorenz's paper "Deterministic Nonperiodic Flow" introduces chaos theory but is largely ignored
1965	Roger Penrose and Stephen Hawking describe the singularity in black holes
1970	John H. Conway's Game of Life is introduced in the pages of *Scientific American*
1972	Lorenz coins the term *butterfly effect* to suggest how tiny changes in initial conditions can create drastically different results
1974	Penrose discovers a new way to tile objects on a surface
1975	Benoît Mandelbrot coins the term *fractal* to describe a new kind of nested structure
1980s	Fractals are popularized in many books, including Mandelbrot's *The Fractal Geometry of Nature;* James Gleick and other writers popularize chaos theory
1987	Christopher Langton organizes the first conference on artificial life at Los Alamos
1988	Stephen Wolfram releases his Mathematica software
1989	Penrose takes on the artificial intelligence community in his book *The Emperor's New Mind*
1990s	The field of artificial life flourishes
1994	Having largely recovered from mental illness, John Nash receives the Nobel Prize in economics for his work in game theory
2002	Wolfram publishes his massive and provocative book *A New Kind of Science*

GLOSSARY

algebra The branch of mathematics that uses letters and symbols to represent known and unknown values

algorithm A detailed procedure for performing a calculation or other task on a computer

Arabic numerals The familiar numerals 1 to 9, plus 0. They were actually invented in India

artificial intelligence The effort to create intelligent behavior in computers or robots

artificial life The effort to simulate biological organisms and eco-systems on the computer. *See also* GENETIC PROGRAMMING

attractor A point or curve toward which a dynamic or chaotic system eventually converges

bell curve *See* NORMAL DISTRIBUTION

black hole An object (such as that resulting from a large collapsed star) that forms a singularity with infinite density and that has intense gravity and a boundary called an event horizon

blinker A pattern in the Game of Life that alternates between two forms

Brownian motion Random movement of small particles in a fluid, caused by jostling of adjacent molecules

butterfly effect Term coined by Edward Lorenz for chaotic systems whose final form varies widely with slight changes in initial conditions. The metaphorical example is the flapping of a butterfly's wings eventually creating a tornado

calculus The branch of mathematics that deals with the relationship between changing quantities, using differentiation or integration

cellular automaton A system where a pattern on a grid is operated on according to certain rules to create a new pattern. Many possible rules exist, and behavior can vary widely

chaos theory   The study of dynamic systems that are deterministic but very sensitive to initial conditions

computer model   A program that incorporates equations describing a process (such as weather) and that can be used to simulate or predict the phenomenon

cooperative game   In game theory, a game in which groups of players are free to form coalitions for their mutual advantage

correlation   In statistics, the degree to which a change in one variable is related to a change in another. The range typically goes from -1 (a perfect inverse relationship) to 0 (no relationship) to 1 (a perfect direct relationship)

dualism   The split (associated with the thought of Plato) between the mind with its ideal forms and the body with its imperfect senses

edge of chaos   Christopher Langton's analysis that interesting, life-like behavior depends on a flow of information that is novel but not chaotic

emergence   The process by which complex structure or behavior arises from a simpler predecessor. This is a key concept for much research in cellular automation and artificial life

eugenics   A theory, popular in the late 19th and early 20th centuries, that tried to apply evolutionary and genetic principles to identify "superior" human genes and encourage their reproduction, while discouraging reproduction by persons deemed to have inferior genes

Fibonacci numbers   A series of numbers introduced to Europe by Leonardo of Pisa. Each number in the series is the sum of the two preceding numbers. The series begins 1, 1, 2, 3, 5, 8 . . .

fractal   A shape that consists of endless layers that appear to have the same structure at every scale. A fractal has a fractional dimension greater than its apparent dimension

Game of Life   A cellular automaton invented by John H. Conway. Thousands of interesting patterns have been discovered

game theory   The branch of mathematics that analyzes strategic choices made by participants in a game, conflict, or bargaining situation

general relativity   The theory developed by Albert Einstein that explains the relationship between mass, energy, and gravity in terms of the shape of space-time

genetic programming A programming technique where competing programs are selected for fitness to perform a task, much as animals are subject to natural selection. Successful programs can have their code combined (simulating sexual reproduction)

glider gun A pattern in the Game of Life that ejects an endless series of objects called gliders. It was discovered by William Gosper

golden ratio A relationship where the smaller part has the same ratio to the larger part as the larger part has to the sum of the two parts. It is frequently found in the dimensions of rectangles, such as in the ancient Greek Parthenon. Numerically, the golden ratio (or golden section) is approximately 0.618

goodness of fit A measure that measures how well a statistical model fits a set of observations. Pearson's chi-square test is a commonly used method to calculate goodness of fit

group theory The branch of mathematics concerned with groups and their possible symmetries. Groups can be used to classify phenomena, such as in physics and chemistry

Incompleteness theorem A theorem proven by Kurt Gödel stating that for any consistent mathematical system, it is possible to construct assertions that are true but not provable using only the rules of that system

kurtosis In statistics, a measure of how far outlying values are from the mean

linear Having an output that varies smoothly and predictably according to the input

Lorenz attractor A particular attractor for a chaotic system that has a butterfly-like shape. *See also* ATTRACTOR

Mandelbrot set A famous and complex fractal discovered by Benoît Mandelbrot. *See also* FRACTAL

Mathematica Software developed by Stephen Wolfram to allow for manipulation of mathematical symbols using methods familiar to mathematicians

matrix A two-dimensional array of numbers that can be manipulated as a unit (such as multiplication)

mean In statistics, the average of a group of values

microtubule A cylindrical protein structure in cells. Roger Penrose believes that microtubules in neurons may be able to use quantum effects to store multiple states or information

Nash equilibrium In game theory, the state in which each player has selected the best strategy in the light of the other's choices. John Nash proved that at least one equilibrium must exist in any finite game with any number of players

natural selection In evolution, the process by which those organisms that have the most suitable traits for survival in a given environment will reproduce and pass the traits to offspring

normal distribution In statistics, the distribution of essentially random data (such as variations in data) is plotted along a bell curve where values cluster near the middle and taper off symmetrically to either side

number theory The study of the properties and relationships of numbers, particularly integers

Penrose tiles A pattern of tiles discovered by Roger Penrose that can cover a space completely but without repeating

Pythagorean theorem The theorem identified with the ancient Greek mathematician Pythagoras. It states that in a right-angled triangle, the square of the length of the hypotenuse (diagonal) is equal to the sum of the squares of the lengths of the other two sides

quantum computer A computer in which each memory location can hold many values at the same time because of a quantum "superposition." In theory, quantum computers would be vastly more powerful than conventional machines

quantum theory The branch of physics that deals with the behavior of objects at the level of atoms and subatomic particles

Renaissance A period in European history characterized by a revival and flourishing of art and architecture and a focus on human nature and capabilities; roughly the 15th and 16th centuries

Roman numerals The ancient Roman system where numbers were assigned to certain letters of the alphabet (such as L = 50 and C = 100). Numbers were aggregated through addition or subtraction rather than using a place value system. *See also* ARABIC NUMERALS

schizophrenia A mental disorder characterized usually by disorganized thinking (the word means roughly "shattered mind") and often by delusions or hallucinations

set theory The branch of mathematics that deals with defining and manipulating groups of abstract objects

singularity In mathematics, a point where a function becomes infinite or undefined. In physics, a point of infinite density where gravity causes infinite curvature, as in a black hole

standard deviation In statistics, a measure of how dispersed a set of data points are; specifically, the standard deviation is the square root of the variance

statistics Collection, organization, and analysis of data using mathematical tools

stored program computer A computer that, like all modern computers, holds program instructions as well as data in memory. John von Neumann is often credited with the concept

strange attractor An attractor in a chaotic system, or that has fractal dimension. *See* ATTRACTOR and FRACTAL

Turing machine *See* UNIVERSAL COMPUTER

twistor A mathematical construct developed by Roger Penrose to describe the behavior of objects or fields in four-dimensional space-time

universal computer A computer that is capable of performing any possible calculation (and thus, of simulating any other type of computer). Alan Turing first conceptualized a universal computer, so it is often called a Turing machine

Vants Simulated ants created by Christopher Langton; they are an example of artificial life

zero-sum game In game theory, a game in which any gain by one player involves a corresponding loss by the other player. Most traditional games (such as chess) fall into this category

FURTHER RESOURCES

Books

Albers, Donald J., and G. I. Alexanderson. *Mathematical People: Profiles and Interviews*. Boston: Birkhauser, 1985.
> A collection of biographical sketches and interviews that bring out interesting aspects of mathematicians' life and work.

Albers, Donald J., G. I. Alexanderson, and Constance Reid. *More Mathematical People: Contemporary Conversations*. Boston: Harcourt, Brace, Jovanovich, 1990.
> Additional interviews focusing on mathematicians who are currently active.

Berlinski, David. *Infinite Ascent: A Short History of Mathematics*. New York: Modern Library, 2005.
> Clearly explains 10 breakthroughs in the history of mathematics, from Pythagoras to Gödel.

Dainitith, John, and Richard Rennie, eds. *The Facts On File Dictionary of Mathematics*. 4th ed. New York: Facts On File, 2005.
> An up-to-date dictionary of mathematical terms and concepts.

Dunham, William. *The Mathematical Universe*. New York: Wiley, 1994.
> An A-to-Z guide to the great concepts and personalities in mathematics.

Gleick, James. *Chaos: Making a New Science*. New York: Viking, 1987.
> Probably the best single account of the development of fractal geometry and the science of chaos, including the work of Mandelbrot and Lorenz.

Henderson, Harry. *Modern Mathematicians*. New York: Facts On File, 1996.
> Includes profiles of 13 19th- and 20th-century mathematicians who worked in a variety of fields.

Levy, Steven. *Artificial Life: The Quest for a New Creation*. New York: Pantheon Books, 1992.
> An engaging account of the researchers who created the field of artificial life in the 1980s and early 1990s.

159

Mathematicians and Computer Wizards. (Macmillan Profiles) New York: Macmillan, 2001.
> Provides biographical sketches of many mathematicians and people in the computer field.

Poundstone, William. *The Recursive Universe.* New York: William Morrow, 1985.
> A classic account of developments in mathematics, computer science, and physics, with an emphasis on cellular automata and Conway's Game of Life.

Yount, Lisa. *A to Z of Women in Science and Math.* New York: Facts On File, 1999.
> A biographical dictionary covering many women who made important contributions to mathematics.

Internet Resources

Convergence. Available online. URL: http://mathdl.maa.org/convergence/1/convergence/1. Accessed on July 24, 2006.
> An online magazine focusing on providing resources for the history of mathematics; particularly geared toward teachers.

The MacTutor History of Mathematics Archive. Available online. URL: http://www-groups.dcs.st-and.ac.uk/~history/index.html. Accessed on May 5, 2006.
> Provides extensive biographies and other background material on the history of mathematics.

Math Archives. University of Tennessee, Knoxville. Available online. URL: http://archives.math.utk.edu. Accessed on July 22, 2006.
> Includes extensive links organized by mathematical topic.

Math Forum. Drexel University. Available online. URL: http://mathforum.org. Accessed on July 24, 2006.
> Provides resources for math students and teachers (through high school).

Mathworld. Wolfram Research. Available online. URL: http://mathworld.wolfram.com. Accessed on July 18, 2006.
> An extensive site with encyclopedia coverage of mathematical topics.

Periodicals

Journal of Recreational Mathematics
Published by Baywood Publishing Company
26 Austin Avenue
Box 337

Amityville, NY 11701
Telephone: (800) 638-7819
   Focuses on puzzles and other kinds of "fun" mathematics

Mathematical Connections
Steve Whittle or Keith Luoma
University College
Augusta State University
Augusta, GA 30904-2200
Telephone: (706) 737-1685
   Explores the relationship between mathematics and the humanities

Math Horizons
Published by the Mathematical Association of America
1529 Eighteenth Street, NW
Washington, DC 20036-1385
Telephone: (800) 741-9415
   A general-interest mathematics publication

Scientific American
415 Madison Avenue
New York, NY 10017
Telephone: (212) 451-8200
   Has coverage of mathematics, including regular columns on recreational mathematics

Societies and Organizations

American Mathematical Society
http://www.ams.org
201 Charles Street
Providence, RI 02904-2294
Telephone: (800) 321-4267

American Statistical Association
http://www.amstat.org
732 North Washington Street
Alexandria, VA 22314-1943
Telephone: (888) 231-3473

Association for Women in Mathematics
http://www.awm-math.org
11240 Waples Mill Road
Suite 200
Fairfax, VA 22030
Telephone: (703) 934-0163

Mathematical Association of America
http://www.maa.org
1529 Eighteenth Street, NW
Washington, DC 20036-1358
Telephone: (800) 741-9415

INDEX

Note: *Italic* page numbers
indicate illustrations.

A

Aiken, Howard 34
algebra, origin of term 5
algorithm 5
animals, Fibonacci num-
bers in 8–9
animation, computer 127
anomalies, in development
of science 83–84
Arabic numerals, calcu-
lating with, v. Roman
numerals 2–3
Arab mathematicians 5
architecture, golden ratio
used in 9, *10*
art, cellular automaton
rules applied to 142
artificial evolution 115,
123, 129–131
artificial intelligence (AI)
artificial life and 131
cellular automaton
rules applied to 142
consciousness and
111–113, 114–115
artificial life
applications of 132
artificial intelligence
and 131
cellular automaton
rules applied to 142
computer as environ-
ment for 120, *130*
computer-simulated
122–123
consciousness and
131–132

development of xvii
recognition as field
129
Artificial Life (Levy) 132
astronomy, fractals in 69
Atomic Energy
Commission, Neumann
in 33
attractors 83, *84*
automaton, cellular
applications of 142
Conway's work on 94
development of 39–40
in Game of Life 94
Neumann's work on
39–40
universality of 140,
141, 142, *144*
Wolfram's work on
138, 139, 140–142
automaton, self-reproducing
development of 37–40
Langton loop 124–126
Langton's work on
124–126
Neumann's work on
37–40, *39*
states of 124
automaton rules, cellular
in nature 140–142,
141
as scientific paradigm
143–146
types of 142–143, *143*
Wolfram's work on
138, 139, 140–146

B

bargaining, game theory
in 49

"Bargaining Problem, The"
(Nash) 49
Beautiful Mind, A (film)
55
Bell, E. T. 46
bifurcation behavior 82
binary, in data storage
36–37
biology
cellular automaton
rules applied to 142,
145–146
fractals in 69, *69*
Biometrika (journal) 21,
24–25
bipolar disorder 53
Bjerknes, Vilhelm 75
black holes
Hawking's work in
109
Penrose's work in 108
Blind Watchmaker, The
(Dawkins) 130–131
Boids (program) 127
Book of Numbers, The
(Conway) 36–37
brain
holistic connectivity
in 113
as quantum computer
113–114, *116*
quantum effects in 114
Breazeal, Cynthia 131
Brief History of Time, A
(Hawking) 109
Brooks, Rodney 131
Browder, Felix 51
Budapest 30
Bugia (Algeria) 1–2
Burks, Arthur 37